Serpentine Wisdom

Serpentine Wisdom

Frank W. Hatfield

VANTAGE PRESS
New York

FIRST EDITION

Published by Vantage Press, Inc.
516 West 34th Street, New York, New York 10001

Manufactured in the United States of America
ISBN: 0-533-10244-8

Library of Congress Catalog Card No.: 92-80322

0 9 8 7 6 5 4 3 2 1

Contents

Introduction

This is a book of theories. In the language of the lawyer, it might be called a book of allegations. In my legal practice I never made an allegation unless I believed I could prove it. Likewise, I believe I could support with facts all of the theories in this book. But facts and proofs obfuscate the picturesque portrayal of theory.

I wrote the book in 1986 and 1987, made major changes in 1988, and, upon deciding to have it published, tightened up and added to its theories. Throughout the entire writing process I would often cite a current event to illustrate a point. But the recent changes neither used nor mentioned events after 1988, nor made any attempt to have the events before that year refer to the present as a fixed date. For the historian, the present is the day the page was written, as noted on each page of the original handwritten manuscript. For the reader, the book's ideas are timeless. Let him, therefore, not waste his time over my allusions to current events. I wrote the book hoping that readers will find ample support for its theories from the experiences of their own lives.

* * * * *

At some time during the life of each of us there passes across the mind the thought that this really could be a better world in which to live and that perhaps one could do something to help make it better. Since the beginning of history, man has hoped to find the better life through his religious and political institutions. This book is a "how-to-do-it" book, specifically, how to have a better world. I pick up the gauntlet that Winston Churchill threw down when he proclaimed democracy the worst form of government, except for every other form of government the world has ever seen. I suggest a better form. I leave this new concept with you. Your response will decide whether my epitaph will be that of my college classmate, who wrote: "God knows I left the world a worse place than I found it, but it wasn't entirely my fault."

Serpentine Wisdom

Chapter I
My Motivation

I am sixty-nine years old and recently retired. Now, at long last, I would like to be happy. This is not to say that I have not always wanted to be happy, nor to say that I have not had moments of happiness or even an occasional happy day. What I am saying is that on balance the unhappy, routine, boring, worthless, and wasted moments of one's life so outweigh the happy moments that one wonders whether the other option, the option against living, would not be preferable. After a moment's reflection, however, one realizes that this other option logically is a nonoption, as one never knows what one would be getting into by electing it and one never knows what unexpected happiness tomorrow may bring.

All that is left for me, therefore, is the task of working at being happy, of implementing happiness, of implementing the dream and the faith of my childhood that the world could be a happy place and that I could leave it a happier place than I found it. The world is most certainly not a happy place or even as happy a place today as it was when I entered it, so my work has been cut out for me.

I do not want to get hung up over the use of words or over the correctness of my historical recollections. I am only interested in giving the reader the benefit of my thinking. I mention the names of others, not as the inebriated man uses the lamppost for support but, hopefully, for light, and in any event so that you may know that I think I did not invent the thought.

I believe it was Thomas Jefferson whose writings first introduced me to the concept of the pursuit of happiness. This was the third of his three inalienable rights of man, following life and liberty. Jefferson had substituted the expression *the pursuit of happiness* for the word *property,* which the practical Englishman Locke had used, and for the word *égalité* (equality), which the more philosophical Frenchman Montesquieu had used in describing the three inalienable rights of man. I do not know what Jefferson meant by "the pursuit of happiness," but I know the happiness in which I am interested cannot be pursued as one pursues pleasure or as one pursues the wily trout, which I can do for only about four days straight before being satiated. The happiness I seek is more a state of mind rather than a pursuit, more a contentedness, a holding together, the state of being held together, content without contention. Perhaps these two poor words from different roots will help you understand the first problem I encounter in working at being happy. I cannot be completely happy until every other person in the world is happy also. How can anyone say he is happy if outside his home at night there may be one unhappy man bent on violence or one starving orphan crying for food?

Maybe you think I have bitten off more than I can chew. Note, however, how restrictive I have already made my task. Not one word has been said of making plants or other animals happy. I am entirely willing to allow flora and fauna to remain under the dominion of man, a concept that I first met in the Old Testament and that assumes a proper stewardship.

No matter what challenge one poses for oneself, one must start at the beginning, but it is often difficult to find the starting point, as any lawyer who has tried to get legal descriptions of metes and bounds off of surveys will tell you. I spent years floundering as a weekend recreational skier until I met Peter Koecke, a ski instructor at Mount Mansfield, Stowe, Vermont. He taught us that the starting point in skiing is always to have your upper body motionless and headed in the direction you want to go. Wouldn't you think learning to use the legs to turn the skis would have been the first step?

I have never read the writings of those credited with having provided the intellectual background for the 1917 communist revolution in Russia and whose aim was to achieve a classless society. I remember our professors at college pointed out how the achievement required the creation of a totalitarian governmental structure with its new class of officialdom. I also remember how our professors laughingly emphasized that the last few pages of these writings concluded, without explanation, that once the classless society had been achieved the state apparatus would wither away. Obviously, a classless society was not achieved. The communists never found the starting point.

Accordingly, I conclude that, as I have set out to make everybody happy, there are two obvious starting points: either I first try to make myself happy or I first try to make others happy. Just to state the alternatives is to make the decision, because how could an unhappy person show another unhappy person how to be happy?

Jack Kennedy, quoting an ancient Greek, said that if you want to be happy, find some activity that has scope, is of benefit to humanity, is capable of being done excellently, and then do it excellently. Using this quotation as a starting point, I shall try to make myself happy. The activity I have chosen is to write this book to show people how to have a better world. If achieved, this would certainly make other people happy. This project could meet all of the Greek's requirements.

Having reached this conclusion, I shall stop using the word *happiness*. *Happiness* is a weak word derived from *hap*, meaning "good luck," as contrasted to *mishap*, meaning "bad luck." So, literally, it would be foolhardy for one to work at being happy since, etymologically, happiness is all a matter of fate anyway. I prefer Shakespeare's approach:

> The fault, dear Brutus, is not in our stars,
> But in ourselves, that we are underlings.

In addition, I shall introduce the next chapter by pointing out that it is axiomatic that one cannot contemplate a better world without talking about governments, whose power to tax is the power to destroy, as Chief Justice Marshall so succinctly wrote.

Chapter II
My Vision

This is a book about the best form of government. Plato said there were only five types of government: (1) an aristocracy, in which the people are ruled by a philosopher king; (2) an oligarchy, in which a few people rule; (3) a timocracy, in which certain people are deemed worthy to rule based on some standard of merit such as ownership of property; (4) a democracy, where the people rule themselves; and (5) despotism, in which a tyrant rules. Plato continues by showing how in history each such form of government by passage of time evolves into the next form. Upon the death of the king, power passes to the chosen few advisors (*oligos* means few), who later have to share their power with the powerful, until the people demand that the power be theirs, and having gotten it lose it, as any mass of cooks would lose the broth, to the strong man who kicks the people out of the kitchen. When the strong man dies, the successor by heredity or by appointment at some point in the succession may be of philosophical bent so that the whole process starts over again with a benevolent despot.

I do not care whether you agree with Plato, or whether you see the contemporary United States as form four or contemporary Russia as form three. Plato is a good starting point and is thoughtful. Now I suggest a sixth form for government.

The thesis of this book is that the best form of government is philosophical anarchy. These two words, derived from four Greek words, mean, stated vulgarly: any person cherishing common sense knows that, in theory, the best form of government is *no* government, because nobody likes to be pushed around.

This book voices the dream that achievement of philosophical anarchy is a rational possibility. All that is needed is that everyone do the right thing voluntarily at all times. Is this thought any wilder than the thought that by having everybody pushing everybody else around at all times, what has been called the divine right of the ballot box, a good government can be achieved? I am not unmindful that such pushing around is relatively far better than that of the tyrant or of war, whose pushing around results in death; but pushing one around nonviolently, a procedure currently in vogue, suppresses the individual, and suppressed individuals do not make for a healthy society.

Dreamers are looked upon as impractical, but this book offers the world the prospect of annual savings of trillions of dollars. Once people accept philosophical anarchy as their form of government, instantly not only has the defense budget been eliminated, but also, what is far more costly, the entire legal system has been eliminated, including the costs of the courts and of educating and providing a living for all that work in or about them and including the savings of time and money of the litigants who have to waste their time in them and of all others who have to try to avoid being in them, not to mention the costs of government itself.

There are, admittedly, two problems in trying to find the answer to the problems of the world in the establishment of universal philosophical anarchy. As such, a society requires everyone to do the right thing voluntarily at all times. First, everyone has to agree on what would be the right thing to do; and, secondly, everyone has to do what is right voluntarily. These are two distinct problems. Of whom did Cicero orate, "He always sees the better way, but he always chooses the worse"? Before these two problems can be tackled, however, the threshold question is, How does one determine what is right? Answering this question is another purpose of this book. After all, if one does not know what he is to agree to, he cannot agree to it; and if he does not know what is right to do, he cannot do it.

When presented with a legal problem, I always seek to find the best past handling of a similar problem, then use it as a model and, hopefully, improve upon it. One never has the time to reinvent the wheel. Besides, the wheel has already been accepted. The best past handling of the problem of determining what is right that I know of is that found in the Old and New Testaments. Eve first poetically gave us this problem by eating of the fruit of the tree of the knowledge of good and evil, thereby forcing us to try to know what is good and what is not. I shall not use the word *goodness,* as I prefer the Elizabethan word *righteousness.*

Jesus of Nazareth also made no attempt to reinvent the wheel. Everything he taught was an improvement on the treatment he found in the Old Testament. He is the only man who ever lived whom I admire without qualification, so perfect a man that I gladly call him God. He is my standard of righteousness, which I make no attempt to improve but only to use in an imperfect way, and my symbol of all the wonderful things I believe in that are invisible to my knowledge. Jesus had his priorities straight. He said, "Seek ye first the kingdom of God and his righteousness and all else shall be added unto you."

He also said, "Be ye wise as serpents and harmless as doves."

Hence, the thrust of this book is serpentine wisdom, in which I use the teachings of Jesus about the kingdom of God to show us the way to achieve the scholar's state of philosophical anarchy, because the concepts are identical. Both states are predicated on the universal voluntary acceptance of what is right. The scholar contemplates that every person in the world will achieve such a degree of wisdom that his actions will reflect what is right for all involved. The Christian contemplates that every person in the world will try to think and do what God would want him to think and do in any situation.

You will note the omission of "the" in the title. I make no claim of having *the* word on serpentine wisdom, I feel uncomfortable in the presence of those who have *the* word on anything, such as *The* Country Club (Boston) or *The* Cricket Club (Philadelphia), so I expect you will feel uncomfortable if at any time I slip and refer to my approach to anything as *the* approach. Let us now proceed to discover what is right for each individual to think and to do in order to have a better world. At this point in the development of our theme, let the believer think of this as a search for the kingdom of God and let the nonbeliever think of this as a search for a form of government better than the world has yet seen.

Chapter III
A Logical Approach

William Penn said he did not care what form the government took—whether monarchy, republic, or other. You will remember it was the form of government with which Plato was concerned. Penn cared about the substance of government, about what government did. Today governments do a great deal. Today governments are needed to enable the individual to try to live in society without conflict. In that the functions of government expand with the increase of the legal sophistication of the society and expand geometrically with the increase in the number of individuals in the society, and as technological advances have increased the interrelationships throughout the entire world, today the potential functions of government are international, infinite, overwhelming, and stifling.

Whenever in the past I have tackled a challenge that is too hard for me, whether it be skiing down too steep an untried slope or trying to find a trout in too large an unknown river, I find it best to try to cut the problem down to manageable size by pretending, for example, I have to get down only the next ten yards if skiing or I have to catch the fish in twenty square yards of water that look like a nice home for trout. So now I shall list the functions of government and then later in the book break them down into bite-size pieces for treatment.

Governments maintain order within the governmental body and protect the body from outside enemies. They manage the household of the body. This includes economic functions such as the money supply, the banking system, the systems for taxation, the regulation of the production of goods and services and of their distribution, and the regulation of investment in the producers and distributors. This also includes environmental functions such as the protection of natural resources from undue consumption and pollution. Governments also provide services such as police and fire protection, postal services, and services relating to the health, welfare, and education of the governmental body.

Remembering my task is to show the way to proceed from an overregulated society to an ungoverned society and remembering my unwillingness to reinvent the wheel unnecessarily, I propose to transfer as many of these functions of government as possible to institutions that are already in existence and in the process to make suggestions for improvement of these institutions. My thrust will be for the institution gradually to take over more and more of the governmental function. Remembering my desire to cut the problem down to a manageable size and realizing that the larger the institution the greater the potential for bad, I propose to discuss the smallest of the important institutions, one that also happens to be the first institution to which each of us belongs, namely, the family. But first let us enjoy a divertissement.

Chapter IV
A Romantic Approach

This chapter is an interlude in the form of an undelivered sermon written years ago by one who grew up in the rectory but never was ordained. It has been included in this book in the hope that its overtones, like those of the song of the Carolina wren, will awaken the imagination of the reader to the grandeur of the concepts with which we are dealing, rather than leave it in drowsiness from the monotonous notes of the last chapter, which, calling upon the private sector for more help, once again, may have sounded like the constantly repeated, ineffective triads of the tufted titmouse—give (pronounced "geeve,") me, give me, give me—give me, give me, give me.

I propose to reaffirm the faith of our tradition by word pictures that I shall paint with my mind. The first word picture consists of two animals, not the proverbial lion and lamb.

Now an exercise of this nature were best accomplished through the use of the Socratic method, whereby the speaker, with impeccable logic, ruthlessly asks a succession of piercing questions until at some point the audience responds with the answer acceptable to his thesis. As I am no Socrates, we shall not use the method, lest those of you whose answers are found acceptable should feel used and those of you whose answers are not found acceptable should feel abused. From time to time, nevertheless, I shall ask a rhetorical question that I will appreciate your answering to yourself in silence so that you may have an opportunity to realize my thesis is agreeable, in the sense at least of being capable of being agreed with.

First animal. What is your favorite animal? Mine is the tiger—so beautiful, so strong, so quiet, the epitome of the loner, of the one who walks alone, of freedom and of independence, the same independence for which man's spirit yearns and the same freedom for which it cries out. You cannot create an artistic masterpiece by appointing a committee.

Second animal. What animal most resembles man? The monkey. Beautiful? Cute maybe, like a baby. Strong? Very iffy, depending on the size. Quiet? No. No. Have you ever watched a group of monkeys at the zoo? It's chatter, chatter, chatter. Laugh at the noise, but do not knock it, for this chattering is their means of survival. It alerts them to real or suspected danger, and together their clamor scares off the intruder.

When I come home after a rough, tough day's workout in the rat race of civilization's businesses and turn on the tube and hear the evening news commentators and their chatter, chatter, chatter, I laugh at it, but I do not knock it, for this is the way public opinion is developed and communicated. This is the way we alert people to real or suspected dangers because man's survival is in the group. Man is a group animal. "No man is an island."

Go alone hungry, thirsty, naked, and empty-handed into the wilderness; how long will you be able to live? How many, not days, how many hours? It is the interdependence of man that requires law and order, organization and institutions, and a harnessing of the spirit in order to fashion a civilized society out of what would otherwise be anarchy. Make no mistake about it: to the extent you are independent, you are not dependent and to the extent you are dependent, you are not independent; and man is and always has been a group animal, dependent, yet with a spirit crying alone in the wilderness of his soul for freedom.

This is the challenge that has confronted the great minds of history. Several hundred years ago an English poet, who in one of his poems shared my love of the tiger, in other writings dramatized the conflict, saying that though energy is eternal delight, still all energy is evil, and all good is restraint. Put your intellectual teeth into this jugular quotation and chew on it. If we are to survive, being dependent, we need the group's togetherness, which today can only be achieved through the law and its rules, regulations, and restraints and which therefore are glorified as goodness; correspondingly we look very carefully when we see in others any indication that they do not consider their energies likewise restrained.

At the beginning of this century Pareto wrote four thick volumes grappling with this same problem of dependence versus independence. He is known as the father of modern sociology, but do not let the big and, at that time, new word lose you. Remember your Latin and your Greek and encourage those who come after you also to learn and remember them. *Socios,* Latin accusative, means "companions." In Caesar's Gallic wars it meant "allies." Today it means "society, one's companions." *Logos* was the Greek word for "word," speech, which distinguishes man from animals. Sociology is the study of one's relationships with one's companions. Pareto concluded that each person has two great and often conflicting needs: a need for a feeling of personal integrity, of being at one with oneself—call it practicing what you believe if you will—and a need for social acceptance, for being accepted by one's companions. Independence versus dependence.

But of all the great thinkers who have observed this conflict the only one who has come up with a solution that has captured my imagination is Jesus, and that is why I am a Christian. Let me see if I can show you Jesus' solution. In order to do so I must start you, not at the beginning, but at the end of my thinking, with a completely arbitrary, dogmatic, humanistic conclusion, which you need not accept. I believe before any society may properly be called a civilization there must be present in it three institutions. Admittedly, a nice civilization would require more institutions. This brings us to our second word picture.

The second word picture consists of nothing more than the word *institution* itself. Lest you find the painting of it offensive, I shall let you paint it for yourself after telling you the meaning of the word. "In" is from the Latin word that has the same meaning in English. The root of the remainder of the word is *sta,* the Latin root for "stand." Institution is where its members all stand in it together.

What is the first necessary institution? What institution did you first find yourself standing in without the faintest notion why? The family. And if you were raised in a Christian family, what was the second institution you again found yourself standing in without the faintest notion why? The church. And the third institution is the community, be it at the local, provincial, national, or international level.

We shall analyze the family, the most uncomplicated of these three necessary institutions. Should you find the exercise naive or immature, I challenge you to transpose my comments in your mind and apply them as we proceed to the organization of the church and of the community, because these concepts are universal.

All of us are or have been children. Many of us are parents. The parents are the leaders of the institution of the family of which parents and children are members. What is the hardest task of the parents, the challenge of their leadership? To feed the children? Not at all. We agree that one function of the parents (and an important one, which we will outline in orderly fashion in the next chapter) is to feed the children physically, mentally, and spiritually. We agree this can be hard to do, but it is not the ultimate in intellectual challenge. What is? Next picture.

Where the boot of Italy kicks the football of Sicily lie narrow straits renowned in all history for the difficulty of the passage, because on the rocky mainland dwelt the mythological creature called Scylla, who by her singing lured the ancient mariners to their destruction against the rocks, while on the other side were the whirlpools of Charybdis, into whose watery depths huge ships were sucked. This is history's most famous difficult passage between extremes. This is the word picture I wish you ever to visualize when thinking of the parents' jugular task, that of lifting the child to maturity without too much permissiveness, without too much independence, lest he destroy himself on the rocks of Scylla, and without too much discipline, too much dependence, lest you drown his spirit in the whirlpool of Charybdis.

We have now arrived at the most important institutional questions. How much permissiveness? How much discipline? How much independence? How much dependence? As I told you that Jesus has the solution, while you are invoking your biblical knowledge to come up with the right percentage, I want to give you an example of one man's percentage.

Von Clausewitz's *Art of War* probably continues to be the classic book on the intellectualizing of war. I am told he points out that one characteristic of the great general is that he realizes his troops always fight better after suffering 20 percent casualties in their last battle. When casualties exceed such percentage they become demoralized; when less, they goof off.

Are you now ready to give me Jesus' percentage? How much discipline? You cannot, because Jesus never answered this most important of man's questions. The amazing paradox is that by not answering it Jesus gave us the only way to live in peace with it unanswered. Once you understand this paradox you have the keys to the kingdom. Are you ready?

The challenge of the passageway between Scylla and Charybdis, between the law and the spirit, is best pictured by two vertical arms representing the law and encompassing the spirit. If they come together they block the spirit's upward ascent toward creative development, and if they separate and fall they give the spirit no structural developmental framework, so that it often destroys itself by crashing upon the rocks. Man's law and man's spirit operate on the same plane and are in competition.

Now take this vertical structure and turn it at right angles so that across the top the horizontal line in all its 100 percent fullness represents God's law as revealed by Moses and the prophets from the beginning to the present and so that at the bottom the horizontal line in all its 100 percent fullness represents man's spirit. Using this pictorial transposition as symbolic of one simple act of faith, note how by voluntary acceptance of God's law without quibble or interpretation, of God's will, of Jesus as master and yourself as slave, you have achieved 100 percent of the benefits of the law, perfect dependence, and 100 percent of the benefits of the spirit, complete independence, and you need no more fear that man's law will ever drown your spirit or that your spirit will ever destroy itself.

Perhaps it will help you understand this concept of voluntary acceptance of God's laws if I show God's laws at work in a very limited situation. I have often asked myself, Why do I climb mountains? Some climbers have answered this question: "Because they are there." Such climbers are either too lazy to try, or too proud to dare, to verbalize their souls. I climb mountains to leave the world down below, its cities, peoples, noises, smells, edifices, mostly ugly, crimes, and other man-made problems; but most of all, I climb mountains to leave behind me man's restraints upon me, the subtlest and the most compelling of which are man's laws, which envelop my daily life from the moment each morning I have to stop at the first traffic light on my way to work until the realization each evening that more than half of that day's earnings are confiscated from me by taxes to support pyramidal government in the name of justice so that I may enjoy food, shelter, and the pursuit of happiness, laws so mangled and manipulated by man that they remind me in variety of the rats the piper piped out of Hamlin town. Would I could pipe the laws away!

So as I cross over the last fence that the high-range cattle cannot pass and see the peaks surrounded by clear blue sky above and dark green forest below, and as I climb higher and my senses take in the scent of the alpine fir, the sight of the multicolored meadows, the flight of the occasional golden eagle soaring majestically over the towering peaks, and the sound of the first trickle of waters that flow downward to form the greatest rivers, I gloat that I am above man's restraints and man's laws.

But I am not above the law. I have replaced man's laws with the few ultimate commands: Do not try to surmount the mountains in a lightning storm or to tread below massive snow cliffs during a thaw, for the penalty may be instant death. Be properly outfitted, for to be unclothed at thirty degrees Fahrenheit in a thirty-mile-per-hour wind is to be thirty seconds from instant death, or something to that effect. These laws are the law that my spirit voluntarily accepts, the law with which I do not care or dare to tinker; and in thus accepting the law, I have found, if I were to verbalize a religion, the holy spirit. I climb mountains to walk with God.

Let us now test our thesis against the thinking of the ages. Crane Brinton, the great intellectual historian, lectured:

> Gentlemen, there are only two ways to look at intellectual history. You are either a romantic idealist or a classical realist. The idealist's view, graphically speaking, is of an ever rising line beginning at the lower left with the dark unlighted night of the cave man and steadily rising to today's fantastic achievements.

I call these achievements the four M's: First, the trip to the moon, science's most impressive development for a man who, at the beginning, could not even make fire by striking two stones together. Next, music, symphonies versus in the beginning barely an "ugh!" Finally, medicine, and miscellany for those whose favorite successes I have ignored. Yet I could never be a romantic idealist when I think also of man's capability for destruction, nuclear and other bombs that could terminate the species.

> The classical realist's view [continued the historian] is of an ever undulating line because all history reveals times when creativity has flourished only to be followed by eras such as today's.

The three creative periods with which I am acquainted were: (1) the golden age of ancient Greece, when man first became a philosopher with Socrates, his pupil Plato, and Plato's pupil Aristotle, (2) the Rome of the Caesars, when man's administrative ability began to be developed, as evidenced by postal service within one week's time within the extremes of the known world, Constantinople to England; and (3) the Renaissance, with its paintings, music, and literature. Yet I could never be a classical realist, believing as he must in a never-ending series of ups and downs, meaninglessness well captured by these words of a poet: Like gnats above a limpid pool on a sultry summer's eve men dance up and down without the faintest notion why. The historian continued:

> Of course, some independent thinkers have their own graphic pattern for life, especially the cultists. Take the religious sects called Christians. They believe in a parabolic approach to life. One top of the parabola represents man when, by reason of his powers of thought, he first attained supremacy over all animals. Then with Adam he fell to nothingness, the bottom of the parabola, only to rise to the other top of the parabola through the grace of the Lord Jesus Christ.

Let us make sure we understand the beautiful, brilliant story of the fall of Adam. Its point was spoken by the serpent. "Eat, Eve," he said, "of the fruit of the tree of the knowledge of good and evil. Why? So that you too may be a God." God created man in his own image. He gave man powers of thought and dominance over all nature, but the ability to see the difference between good and evil, between right and wrong, came because of the serpent. Have you not in weak moments looked at tax evaders and thought to yourself, *How I wish I were as conscienceless as they?* Well, that was the power thinking man had over animals before Adam. I like to think God, the personification of righteousness, which simply means seeing the difference between right and wrong and then doing the right, felt sorry for imperfect man and so did not himself want to impose upon man the task of righteousness. Hence with Adam man fell to nothingness, because by definition knowing the difference between right and wrong and being imperfect, he could not but fail. In his institutional leadership, in his relationships with others, he would either invoke the strong arm of man's law and to that extent destroy another's spirit or, by doing nothing, by permissiveness, by avoiding the problem, he would allow others to crash against Scylla's rocks. So man was damned if he did and damned if he didn't and "there is no health in us" save through the redeeming grace of Jesus. "Follow me," Jesus says to each generation. We know his two commands: "Love God first and your neighbor as yourself." Do we also know his priorities for us? "Seek ye first the kingdom of God and his righteousness," he said. This, I humbly suggest, is what we have been doing in this exercise, because a kingdom is another name for an institution. Once we realize we cannot solve the problem of all earthly institutions, the problem of balancing dependence and independence, without hurting people and once we voluntarily subject our will to God's law and thereby set our spirit free, the kingdom is at hand.

Together we have now witnessed the pageant of the word pictures, of two animals, tiger and monkey, of the world's institutions where we all stand in it together, of Scylla and Charybdis, of the vertical and the horizontal law, of the graphic patterns of ascending linear line, undulating line, and parabolic curve, and now the last word picture, the broken inkwell.

Who was the last great Christian? While you are thinking, let me mention a wonderful sermon that was preached in Philadelphia early in the 1970s by a British theologian, Dr. Christopher Evans, on St. Paul's Day. "There is," he preached, "a time bomb in Paul's letter to the Romans that has ticked throughout the centuries and about every five hundred years it explodes, first in Augustine, then Aquinas, and lastly in Martin Luther. Hopefully it will explode in you."

Martin Luther was the monastery's privy cleaner. Have you ever cooked for more than family? Cleaned up for more? Luther was seeking the kingdom, and the priestly leadership told him his cleaning job was to be his good work, his key to the kingdom. This same leadership allowed the rich to avoid any necessity for good works by payment of money. Even worse, this leadership granted the rich the privilege to do bad works by payment of money to atone for sins already committed (special indulgences). Indeed, so greedy was the leadership, they let the rich buy atonement for sins yet to be acknowledged or committed (general indulgences), comparable to Ford's pardon of Nixon. So when Luther read Romans, chapter 3, and heard Paul saying "no" to the law and "yes" to the spirit, Luther realized that man's law, the church's law, was destroying his spirit and the spirit of others. He threw the inkwell at the devil he imagined he saw on the wall and reestablished the doctrine of justification by faith in lieu of good works. He realized that good works spring from faith as day from night. This doctrine, I submit, involves nothing more than what our exercise has taught us. Once we voluntarily accept God's law by faith in it as the only solution to the conflict in man resulting from his yearning for independence while realizing dependence is necessary for survival, we have found the keys to the kingdom.

Now, ladies and gentlemen, there is the solution, the answer to all our problems today, and as all signs round you show, it is time for the time bomb to explode again. It is nearly A.D. 2000. Will you be the next great prophet in a long and honorable tradition?

* * * * *

Here I would like to add four postscripts:

To those interested in numerology, which I am not, I would point out that the learned divine may have emphasized the 500-year intervals because of Dante. Dante believed a great leader came along every 515 years because 515 in his Roman numerals is DXV and *dux* means "leader" in Latin.

Secondly, some time after writing the above sermon I was surprised and pleased to read in a review of a biography of Luther that he once wrote his father: "Churches, Kings and fathers—why do they ask so much, and why do they all of them get so much more then they deserve?"

Thirdly, in checking and double-checking my material before publication I read a reprint of Dr. Evans's sermon and was surprised to see added to the list of theologians, after Martin Luther, today's Karl Barth, about whom I have more to say later in this book.

Finally, you ask, How does this sermon of yours fit into our project? Here are the steps. We are seeking a better world. The logical ultimate solution is philosophical anarchy. The need for government, however, is not just going to wither away by our asking voluntary institutions to take over the functions of government. Two factors are needed that thus far in history have not been offered by

philosophy but only by religion. These two fa
a universally accepted standard of righteousne
universally practiced living faith. The purpos
chapter, this sermon, is to give you an insight i
factors. I see the hope of the world in the fulf
the spirit of every man. Law and government
that spirit. Man as child needs the presence of th
law of the parent while he develops his own la
spirit. Society, likewise, needs for the foreseea
the presence of government while its member
their own law-abiding spirit. Eventually, just as
hopefully will one day no longer need parental c
so the spirit of every man hopefully will one day
fulfillment solely through the help of voluntar
tions.

Chapter V
The Family

In the make-believe state of Ames, if a person dies leaving assets of $1,000 or less without leaving a will, a statute enables any debtor of the decedent to satisfy his debt by making payment to the next of kin without requiring an administration of the decedent's estate or court proceedings, provided the next of kin furnishes his (their) affidavit certifying that the decedent died leaving an estate of $1,000 or less, that the decedent died without leaving a will, and that the affiant(s) is (are) the only heir(s) of the decedent. In the classroom discussion of this statute the professor asked the law student; "If a debtor makes payment of $10,000 owing to a decedent's estate to one who gives such an affidavit and if the debtor does so without requiring the administration of the estate or court proceedings, how much does the debtor risk losing if the affiant turns out not to have been the rightful heir?" The student replied, "Ten thousand dollars."

The professor agreed and continued; "What if the debtor owed the estate only $1,001 and made payment to such a false affiant; what then is the debtor's risk?"

The student replied, "One dollar."

"Wrong," said the professor. "The risk remains the same, namely, $1,001, the amount paid. The statute does not apply as the value of the estate exceeds $1,000."

The student learned that in logic the answer remains the same regardless of the amount involved. For this reason I shall treat the institution of the family thoroughly despite the small number of people in each unit because the concepts I develop with respect to the family shall later be used for larger institutions.

Any institution has a membership, a purpose, and an organizational structure. Let us consider a family with a father, a mother, and two children, with the father married to the mother. I like having two children because I think it is the fairest arrangement. It allows for one-on-one relationships. A single child risks having two-on-one situations more frequently, to his detriment. With more than two children, the parents are outnumbered, frequently to the detriment of all. More importantly, I value the concept of sharing between children and I fear overpopulation. Recently Mexico City had an earthquake that killed about 3,000 people, a monstrous catastrophe. Yet with a population of 18 million, if one assumes a life expectancy of fifty years and if my mathematics is correct, 3,000 people is only three days' worth, as it takes 1,000 births daily to maintain such a population. I was once told that each Western steer needs sixteen acres of grazing land for survival. Should each man have less? But I have digressed, as the number of children is a matter of taste, provided the parents are able to fulfill their functions in the family institution.

The purpose of the family is to raise and protect the children and to take care of their needs. These needs are threefold: physical requirements of food, clothing, shelter, and exercise and medical care for a healthy body; mental requirements for the development and education of the mind; and spiritual requirements for the development of the soul. The concept of the soul is a tough one, the explanation of which at this point I think would be premature. These requirements are fulfilled by the parents until the child is able to fulfill them either by himself or with the help of others or other institutions.

The organizational structure of the family brings up Plato's concern about the form of the structure. William Penn to the contrary, I believe the form of government is important. What form then should the government of the family take? Democracy is not feasible, as children cannot have equal votes with parents. Personally I prefer what was called a constitutionally limited monarchy in Tudor England or a federal system as espoused by Hamilton in the *Federalist Papers,* in each of which there is a voice of authority, monarch or president, subject to a multitude of checks and balances in the hands of practically everybody to some and varying degree. I believe any institution must be able to speak with authority or else it will not be able to perform its functions, and in the family I believe the father should be the acknowledged leader for the following reasons, which I list in order of importance:

1. The father has traditionally been the leader. "That you may have a peer in your house" is an old Italian curse.
2. A two-headed rule, as its name implies, is a monster.
3. Historically the father has been the breadwinner, whose work makes the institution self-sufficient and enables the mother, unsullied by direct contact with the business world, to fulfill the primary purpose of the family, the production and raising of the children. Accordingly, the father, whose time is spent primarily at work outside the home, if he does not have the position of leadership, with its corollary duties, may

feel unneeded and pay no attention to the children to their detriment.

By now you readily see I have no absolute standard to use in determining which parent rightfully should govern. Jesus never married. He never discussed this point. Jesus was not an institutional man. Any member of an institution loses something of himself to the institution, but God cannot be limited by man or institution. Jesus castigated institutions, including the family. So I am on my own in thinking one can work to destroy the institution of compulsory government by trying to improve the voluntary institutions in society and the better the leader of an institution does his job, the less the institution is needed and the sooner the leader is out of a job.

4. This brings me to my fourth reason for wanting the father to be the leader of the family. I think it is right—not because the father is necessarily the stronger or the wiser or the better leader, but because in substance it is no big deal who is leader, while in form, as a model or as a witness for others, it is tremendously important who is leader. Only when a society universally values the concept of father as leader can it make an effective witness to the sad, fatherless families in today's urban ghettos and elsewhere and to those well-to-do and other families who spend their time bickering over who should be leader even unto divorce.

Remembering that we have far more difficult problems in human relations to surmount if we are to do away with compulsory government, I respectfully submit that this discussion merits no more space than that taken up by this simile in the style of Virgil: as in one Old Testament battle between mighty armies victory went to that army whose soldiers drank their water from the stream by standing and lapping it up using the palms of their hands as ladles, because the other army's soldiers lay on their bellies sipping up the water with their mouths with the result that they did not see the enemy, so should the father be the ruler of the family if only because in this yet uncivilized world he can have a rifle at the ready and urinate at the same time.

As my cavalier dismissal of this subject will offend the parlor folk who consider themselves more civilized than the rest of the world, I shall dramatize my feelings that this problem in substance is no big deal. Let us suppose that the mother demands what she calls joint rule, saying anything less would diminish her. I assume that by joint rule is meant talking the problem over (and probably over and over) until the parents reach a common decision, whereupon one is allowed to be the spokesman. If one cannot at least be spokesman we have other problems, which are answered by the next paragraph's homely diversion.

The Staten Island ferry is a wonderful tradition. For many years it used to cost just five cents to cross New York Harbor. During rush hours the service is so frequent that the outgoing ferry no sooner prepares to leave one slip than an incoming ferry in another slip, having disgorged its passengers, is ready to take on its next load. All this takes place amidst mass confusion as multitudes of passengers rush up the steps to see which slip is open for loading. This particular morning at Staten Island, two parents rushed up the stairs barely behind two vigorous children whose ages were not yet in the double digits. It was their first trip to the big city. One child and one parent rushed to get in one slip where the attendant was just about to close the gate, and the other child and other parent rushed to get in a slip that had just been opened and was separated from the first slip by a long, high wall. Each parent screamed, "This way!," but the parent whose authority was recognized by the entire family repeated the scream, whereupon the entire family followed. Obviously neither way was better than the other, but being together and not losing each other in Manhattan was important. Note that even had both parents done the obviously polite thing in the situation by following their first screams of "This way!" with simultaneous second screams of "That way!," unless one voice is recognized as authoritative, leadership fails.

Now let us return to the situation where the mother demands joint rule. I cannot answer this demand logically. The lifelong commitment of marriage is not a logical concept. A reasonable man does not give up his options. So I escape to the faith of my fathers and to the wisdom of the ages and bring in, apologetically, the element of mystery, *mystery* from the Greek word for "to close or be shut" to human understanding, and create a leadership of two persons, blessed binary rule. The common law of England comforts me with its delightful fiction of tenancy by the entireties. When husband and wife own land as tenants by the entireties, they each own the whole. Rest assured, I understand what I have just done. In order to maintain the institution, in order to keep a leadership, if only a mere spokesmanship, I let this happen: when my wife and I fail to reach a common decision after talking it over longer than the problem merits, and if a decision may no longer be postponed, she rules.

But I repeat, this is no big deal. I shall use a business concept to illustrate my point. In business when two corporations enter into a joint venture, the Chinese characters for which expression mean "same bed" and "different dreams," the partners have to make long-term commitments to each other. Some lawyers believe open-ended commitments are not proper, as they deprive future boards of directors of their ongoing right and duty to manage the corporation. An open-ended commitment is one the amount or cost of which is not fixed. A commitment to fund the deficits of the venture for twenty years is open; a commitment to lease a property for twenty years for a fixed rent is not open. Note that the long-term commitment of marriage need not be considered an open-ended commitment to the extent that each committing party takes the time before entering into the commitment first to know himself and then to know (*not* in the Old Testament sense) the other, for such knowledge tends to let each know in advance the nature of the demands that are likely to be made upon him. You ask, "How can I know myself?" I would suggest that the best starting point is to get a liberal-arts college degree studying subjects such as literature, history, languages, philosophy, government, and economics, the subjects that deal with man's relationships with man. I would add that everyone must have such knowledge and more before government can be dispensed with.

In conclusion, the parents have the duty of seeing to it that the child develops physically, mentally, and spiritually and of disciplining the child and keeping the family together in the process. To the extent that each can do all of this without pushing the other members of the family around, to that extent each is moving the family toward the kingdom. Note also that this chapter, dealing as it does with our first institution, has an exceedingly joyful ending. Regardless of whether the institution performs its function or not, it has an inbuilt guaranteed withering away of its governmental structure within a time span no longer than one generation. Only too soon do we see our families as yesterdays.

The astute reader will notice I have made no attempt in this analysis of the family to tackle what I have previously called the jugular problem of how much discipline the children should be subjected to and how much permissiveness the children should be allowed. The reasons are: I do not know and I no longer need to know. Family counselors abound for those who do. I also sidestep this problem for the leadership of the two remaining institutions. My whole thesis is that the church should be entirely and solely permissive and the government should be entirely and solely disciplinary.

Now let me use the joy that comes when the institutional aspect of the family withers away upon the children's leaving the nest to show the proper perspective for what is to come. Isaiah tells us a thousand years are but as yesterday in God's sight. Curiously, this ratio is about the same as the ratio of the date of the appearance of land in the earth's firmament to the date of the first known artistic creations of man. Geologists today believe land appeared about 4.8 billion years ago. Fine arts scholars today believe the first cave paintings were painted about 11,000 B.C. Let us, therefore, continue our search for the kingdom by trying to view all our institutions as yesterdays.

Chapter VI
A Voluntary Community

In the last chapter we noted that every institution has a membership, a purpose, and an organizational structure. It was reasonably easy to determine the membership of the family, but this is not so when it comes to the membership of the community. We saw how difficult interrelationships can be within the small membership of the family, and we can imagine how much more so they would be in larger groups. So using the approach of biting off a little bit at a time, I am tempted to develop as the next institution one involving a somewhat greater number of people, such as a clan or tribe, and then to follow this up with increasingly larger institutions along ethnic, religious, or political lines, such as cities, provinces, and nations. I resist this approach, because all history shows its futility in seeking the kingdom. The most that could be hoped for in using such an approach would be for the nations of the world to unite against a mass invasion of creatures from outer space, just as fighting tribes unite only when faced with a foreign enemy. I do not want this exercise of mine to be dependent on such a phenomenon. Rather, with broad brush I shall start where we must end and then try to fill in the supporting pieces. We need a voluntary worldwide community whose membership embraces everyone.

Perhaps another story may help you understand why we need a universal community. Before I married, a wonderful older boy, a friend and a theosophist, showed me why I was failing at the dating game. He said, "You hit them head on. You ask them, 'What college and church do you go to,' et cetera, et cetera? And, of course, they back off. In order for two people to come together they should talk about something outside themselves." Then his hands illustrated his point by depicting two curves, the name for which on a graph I used to know over fifty years ago. His outstretched hands started coming together as though two people were approaching each other on a horizontal axis, but instead of banging into each other at its intersection with the vertical axis, they curved every so gradually upward until together they swept to meet at infinity. Any group, to be cohesive, must have a unifying concept outside itself.

Our wheel for such a worldwide community with its unifying concept outside itself is already in place. It is the dream that has been held over the centuries by every Christian, the dream of one holy catholic and apostolic church. What better vehicle to sweep people upward together toward an unknowable meeting place? Let us consider one by one the words: *one, holy, catholic, apostolic,* and *church.* The word *church* is usable because it refers to the body, that is, the community that holds the beliefs represented by the modifying adjectives. The word *catholic* is usable because it means universal. The word *apostolic* (pertaining to an apostle) will take a little interpretation, because *apostle* means "sent forth" (from some outside source). The word *holy* is not objectionable in that it means whole in a spiritual sense, although the word *spiritual* will need some development; and the word *one* is just what we need—one worldwide community in which everyone wishes to and does apply for membership and from which no one is rejected. Jesus explains the oneness by the story of the one lost sheep. You will remember that the shepherd left the flock unattended to look for one stray. Any general who did this would properly be court-martialed. When government takes the form of philosophical anarchy the chain is no stronger than its weakest link, so universal membership is essential.

I use a universal church as my model for a voluntary community because Christianity is the only religion with which I am acquainted. I have no objection if you want to use another religion or another unifying concept having an unknowable outside source, provided it has the same attributes as Christianity. If the religion or concept you desire to use provides for the same membership, the same purpose, a similar organizational structure, and the same standard of voluntary righteousness, then I would gladly accept its use, as I would expect you to accept my choice. There can be only one religion or concept used, however, in order to have an absolute standard and a uniform determination of righteousness toward which the community can sweep along together.

As in the family, the purpose of a voluntary community is to take care of the needs of its members to the extent that the members cannot take care of their own needs. As in the family, these needs are threefold: physical, mental, and spiritual. As in the family, a voluntary community must have an organizational structure; but before looking into this let us develop a meaning for the expression *spiritual needs,* a concept that we left undeveloped in discussing the family.

Preliminarily, we all know I do not know what I am talking about when I try to define anybody's spirit, including my own, but neither does anybody else, including any divine. This comment is not a put-down but a definitional point. With my mind I know just so much, and a good day is one in which I learn more than I forget. The sum total of knowledge is the total of what everyone knows. That which is not known is what the spirit is all about. It is amazing how throughout history we have had so many professed experts in this realm. It reminds me of the person at the small dinner party who starts pontificating about something only after first assuring himself that none in the group knows anything about the subject matter.

Since by definition the spiritual is not knowable, why do we not just ignore it, which would obviously be the rational approach? Why not follow Mark Twain's approach: the body is mortal and material; the soul is immortal and immaterial? The reason we have to deal with the spirit is that without it we would have nothing more than 4 billion selves, all predatory animals, egocentrically expressing ourselves with a view toward survival. There is needed, therefore, a humbling, unknowable, unifying force outside ourselves toward which together we can aspire and by which we can be inspired. Without such a mystery, to conceive of each self agreeing on what is right, even if all agreed to follow the teachings of Jesus as the standard of righteousness, is not thinkable. One can rationalize any action. I remember the peacetime pacifist who became the wartime soldier, saying, "I can show greater love for my enemy by killing him and risking the everlasting consequences of my behavior rather than by letting him kill me, for then he would surely go to hell, from which awful plight my unselfish act saves him." Hence for the moment I must leave logic and enter the field of faith.

Spirit comes from the Latin word for "to breathe" and indicates that someone has breathed life into each of us—someone outside our knowledge. *Apostle* means "sent forth from a source outside ourself." If I did not consider myself to be an apostle I would not be writing this book. This outside source has been called God since earliest times and has power that man has not yet harnessed, so God is both to be feared and to be loved. I believe in one God, the center of my life, one only, for the same reason that a circle has only one center. I also believe God is a person different from each of us in three ways: (1) as the God I have just mentioned who made everything originally and still is in control; (2) as Jesus, the Christ, the perfect man whom I have already mentioned I accept as God; and (3) as the holy spirit, whose help we seek in order to find out and do what is right based upon what Jesus would want us to do. This process is called trying to follow the will of God. Note that I do not possess the truth. I seek the truth, but the truth remains absolute, though my expression of it is relative and imperfect.

We are now ready to discuss the organization of a worldwide community, which we may often call the church. Again, we need not reinvent the wheel, because the organization is in place. In my opinion the Roman Catholic Church (henceforth called Rome) has the best leadership and the best organization of any large institution in the world today. Historically, I think Rome is probably the oldest institution in the Western world. Its form of government is especially suited for a voluntary community to which no one is forced to belong and to which no one is forced to pay dues or taxes but to which all may belong. Rome is a hierarchy whose authoritative leader is elected for life by certain of those overseers who had been appointed by the leader's predecessors and whose district organizations are controlled by these overseers and others appointed by the leader.

Let us see how adaptable this form of organization would be for fulfilling the purpose of a worldwide community, remembering that the purpose is to take care of the needs of its members. First is the physical requirement. Meeting the physical needs of the people has been a major concern to Christians ever since Jesus commanded the twelve disciples to feed the hungry, clothe the poor, and heal the sick. To the extent that anyone cannot provide for himself and his dependents food, clothing, shelter, and medical care, to that extent the church historically has tried to furnish these requirements. Where the church has failed it has usually failed for lack of funds. When the kingdom comes to earth, thereby relieving me of confiscatory income taxes in excess of 50 percent of my earnings, I am confident I and others once again can keep Jacob's bargain with God and voluntarily tithe to the church 10 percent of our income so that the necessary funds will be available, and I am confident Rome has the spiritual and street wisdom to perform this function of fulfilling the physical requirements of the needy.

The next requirement is that of the mental needs of the members of a voluntary worldwide community. Here Jesus does not show the way, perhaps because there is no correlation between intelligence and righteousness. I remember how Felix Frankfurter was unwilling to waste his time teaching any of us at law school who were not honor students, how when he was appointed to the Supreme Court of the United States he took one of his students to be his law clerk (the happy hot dog), how that student several years later, after leaving Washington, got caught stuffing a ballot box in seeking his own election as a petty magistrate in a southern city, and how the attitude of the law school was that the poor lad should have learned his morality in Sunday school as a child. But if serpentine wisdom means anything, it means having the option to benefit from an intellectual education without benefit of clergy. So here I make the first of my three major suggestions to Rome who, as historic masters of loving and not-so-loving intimidation, will understand these suggestions are to be followed if their branch of the church is to be used as the vehicle for my voluntary worldwide community:

Let those who want to use private secular institutions of education not be asked to contribute toward the parochial school costs, and let those members who want to provide scholarships for those who cannot afford private secular school tuition be given a modest credit toward their voluntary tithing. I say "modest credit" lest one believe erroneously he may earmark his entire voluntary contribution for use in private secular education. Remember the purpose of the church is to fulfill those needs of its membership that the members cannot take care of themselves or through others. I would expect most of the costs of parochial schools would be met by the users of the schools and tithing funds would only be used for the costs attributable to those students whose parents are unable to pay the parochial school costs in addition to their voluntary general tithing. It is with respect to this limited amount that the modest credit would be given.

Incidentally, I reject the concept that compulsory public school education is a civil right. I believe the concept is only about 150 years old, born in New England, and I believe this is one present function of government that can readily be dispensed with. If Harvard can boast, as it does, that no applicant is rejected for lack of funds, we certainly need not wait until the millennium for enough others to make the same boast so that all wishing an education can be accommodated.

The last requirement is that of the spiritual needs of the members of a voluntary worldwide community. Several pages ago I suggested that the essence of Christianity was a belief in a triune God as embodied in Jesus, who shows us how God loves us and what God wants us to do. I have confidence that Rome can fulfill the spiritual needs of the community and can teach its members on a continuing basis that to follow the way of Jesus is the only solution to man's problems. Hence just as we saw that the family is adaptable as an institution to provide for the physical, mental, and spiritual needs of the children, so I believe a church such as Rome is adaptable to provide these needs for its members.

You will remember that, in addition to fulfilling needs, the parents as leaders of the family were required to protect and discipline the children and to maintain the institution. It is in this area of protection, discipline, and institutional maintenance that one may expect to have major problems with Rome, into some of which we shall now delve.

The thinkers who provided the intellectual background for our democracy verbalized a concept that we now call the separation of church and state. This concept, as is true of all controversial concepts, means different things to different people, and more fire than light is shed on the concept, because people do not go back to basics. The institution of government is a mandatory institution whose primary purpose in today's pluralistic society is to protect man from his fellowman through the use of sanctions. The institution of the church is a voluntary institution whose primary purpose is to seek the kingdom through the holy spirit, and when the kingdom comes there will be no need for the sanctions of government. Until the kingdom comes, we need both institutions, but each should mind its own business. The state should neither help nor hurt the church. The church should neither help nor hurt the state. Examples of these four different types of no-nos are:

1. The state should not help the church by giving it subsidies or tax exemptions;
2. The state should not hurt the church by interfering with its activities, unless they are contrary to general civil law, such as the church's offering sanctuary to illegal aliens;
3. The church should not help the state by supporting any of its policies or those of any political group, as laws are enforced by sanctions contrary to the way of Jesus; and
4. The church should not hurt the state by telling it how to perform its functions, such as by telling it what military weapons to use.

This separation of church and state should be both a direct and an indirect separation. For example, the church should tell its membership when it believes the state is defying the laws of God or unnecessarily usurping functions that the voluntary community should be handling. The church should tell its membership where it believes Jesus would stand on a particular political issue. The church should not tell its membership how they should act on any issue under the political exigencies of the particular moment in time. And the church should not itself speak to the state except as required to prevent the state's interference with ecclesiastical activities. Now I shall try to illustrate this concept of separation of church and state by discussing the explosive issue of abortion, which currently is a legal procedure.

Abortion, of course, is spiritually wrong. Note how I accept the leadership of Rome in matters of interpreting the faith. But what the state does about abortion is none of the church's business. Jesus did not go to Caesar saying, "I have a wonderful spiritual message, but people have ears and hear not, so make them practice what I preach." Each member of the church as a citizen should determine his own position on whether or not to outlaw abortion based on political considerations. Note the issue is not whether the member would herself have an abortion. This issue will be discussed later. One entirely reasonable political consideration is that we already have far too many laws, so why not first follow the example of King Hammurabi and pass a law providing for the death penalty for anyone who proposes a law that does not pass? Another political consideration is that in a world torn by war and poverty, life is cheap and resources limited, so that we probably should try to feed and educate those who have already seen the light of day, made friends, and found acceptance in their neighborhoods. The sequel to this consideration is to let the unwanted children die. I am reminded of the story told by an overzealous etymologist. "Genuflection" (flexing the knee) comes, he said, from the same source as "gene," "genesis," and "generation" (to be born). In the days when the Mongolian hordes swept westward it was the custom upon the birth of a child for the father to take it to the ledge overlooking the camp's garbage heap, place it on his knee, look it over very carefully, and keep it only if he saw no imperfections or impediments to their journeys. Only those who passed the knee test made the genealogy. I have said the number of children parents have is a matter of taste, provided they can take care of their children's needs. In a pluralistic society parents should have available all legal options to implement in their discretion this proviso. Hence my second suggestion to Rome is that it cease and desist from using or attempting to use the secular mandatory government for its purpose, as this practice is delaying the coming of the kingdom. The end does not justify the means. You cannot have the kingdom until you abolish mandatory government.

As my cavalier dismissal of this subject will offend the hierarchy, let me repeat my perspective for the benefit of the reader. First, the issue has little to do with logic. My premises can be used to destroy my position easily. I can do it in five steps:

1. A purpose of the church is to fill the needs of its members.
2. The membership should include everyone in the world.
3. Abortion is wrong.
4. The state should not interfere in the affairs of the church.
5. Yet I let the state limit the membership of the church by depriving the church of the ability to convert those who ought to have been born.

My conclusion is that arguing about abortion is time misspent. Abortion is a political issue today to be decided using the test of what is necessary rather than that of what is logical or right. The question of outlawing abortion, like all issues, should be looked at from its effect on the quest for the kingdom. The kingdom is the form of government in which the people follow the will of God by their own volition rather than the will of their fellowman by compulsion. The church properly interprets the will of God to the people, but the church properly does not enforce the will of God. At today's stage of development, mandatory secular government is required to enforce laws as necessary, but it is the challenge of the church in seeking the kingdom to see how many of these man-made and man-enforced laws can be rendered unnecessary. In reading about the creation of our constitution nearly 200 years ago, in 1787, the first written constitution in the history of the world, I am intrigued by how many of its authors emphasized that self-government would not be possible without a virtuous people. I hope by now you perceive more self-government in the kingdom than you find in today's democracy.

This discussion leads us to our next point. Since we are contemplating that Rome will be a model for our voluntary worldwide community, how much internal discipline may her leaders impose upon her members? As our search is for a society in which all agree upon what is right and then do it voluntarily, the only condition for membership therein is belief in the triune God and acceptance of Jesus' standards for righteousness. In other words, each member should accept Jesus as lord and savior and thereby agree to try to follow the will of God. Do not let the word *lord* turn you off. The word is derived from two old Anglo-Saxon words meaning "keeper of the bread." As used in the church, *lord* means "master." It is the type of word that is used with another word as its corollary, for example, master and servant, and this helps one understand its meaning. Beyond such limited acceptance I see no need to require, and much harm from requiring, the membership to accept more that the leadership thinks about matters of faith, that is, to accept further dogma. The word *dogma* comes from the Greek word for "to think." Personally, I have no objection to Rome's dogma. After all, as God cannot be limited, by definition anything is possible unless man knows it is not and dogma is not within man's knowledge. If Rome would say to her voluntary worldwide membership:

> We are your spiritual leaders. Our responsibility is to serve God and propagate the faith, not to meet your needs except as so doing reflects the will of God. The dogma of the church has been developed over the years very carefully and has kept the faith alive thus far. We are not about to risk destroying the faith by dispensing with these holy mysteries now, but we will not penalize members who do not wish to accept them.

If Rome would take this approach, I would pass over the issue. But the Rome that even today is willing to impose its will on a pluralistic society to protect the flock can be expected to insist on disciplining the flock, to which philosophers cannot be expected to take kindly. Just as at times in history secular governments have survived by alliances between rulers and the poor without the support of the middle class, so in our search for the kingdom we may have a chance for success if we can capture the imagination of the wise and the good without, at first, the support of the masses that are spiritually indifferent. So let us again try to achieve a compromise.

The thinkers who provided the intellectual background for the Russian Revolution in 1917 dismissed Christianity as the opium of the people. We can count on philosophers likewise to dismiss Christianity. So before we can expect them to accept the leadership of Rome, we must seek out this opium and eliminate any mandatory requirement for its use by members of the voluntary community. The opium is found, I believe, primarily in two concepts: that of the next world and that of the mysteries, especially miracles and sacraments. The Russian thinkers wanted a better life for all on the earth, just as I do. They viewed the emphasis that the church places on these mysteries as, at best, a cheap and harmless opium that the priesthood kindly offers to the ignorant poor after a tough week's work, in the same fashion that the rich man offers himself his evening martinis after a tough day's work, and, at worst, as an interference with their plans for a better world here and now. From my point of view Rome's emphasis on and her tying together of sacraments and salvation present an aspect of her compulsions that is more insidious than her lack of respect for the doctrine of the separation of church and state. When Rome tries to push the state around, everybody opposed has no option but to fight back; when Rome pushes her membership around, only the membership is affected and it has the option of leaving, so the issues do not get a full and open testing in the marketplace of the world's ideas. For that reason, and without interfering with Rome's authority to interpret matters of faith or to prescribe requirements for the priesthood, I suggest as my third improvement that Rome condition membership and participation in the affairs of the voluntary worldwide community, including participation in the holy mysteries, only upon acceptance of Jesus, as previously indicated. Specifically, for example, if a member wants to have an abortion she may, but not in a church hospital. If a member wants to divorce his spouse, he (by now you realize I use the masculine to include the feminine when the text requires such usage as here) may, and he may remarry, but not in a church ceremony during the lifetime of the divorced spouse. A member does not have to be baptized to become a member or even to receive Holy Communion. Holy Communion may not be required nor may it be withheld except for nonacceptance of Jesus.

If any Jesuit causist or arrogant predestinarian accuses me of bastardizing the faith in an attempt to attract the philosophers of the world, let him reread my chapter on the family, in which in order to keep the entire family together I risked losing my leadership to another. If any philosopher laughs at my feeble attempt to seduce him into believing what he does not know and into giving up his pridefully selfish, wonderful, personal integrity, let him ask himself what he is doing to seek the kingdom and to feed the hungry and heal the sick, other than passing the buck to others through mandatory governmental processes, democratic, communistic, or otherwise. I find revolting such detachment and lack of sympathy, sensitivity, and respect for others. It is the same feeling I had when I first saw the painting, which you may remember as a liquor advertisement, that shows the decorated Napoleon sipping brandy with the colorful enemy generals before the Battle of Marengo. There is not even an appearance of a thought about the kids who would be killed moments later. It is the same feeling I think others have when they behold a famous lawyer's fighting passionately one day on one side of an explosive issue and the next day in another case on the other side of the same issue. Verily, the philosopher is part of the problem. Lest any scientist feel omitted, it is the same feeling I have when I recollect how the nuclear arms race started between the major powers. Some of you will remember the smug self-centeredness that allowed the German scientific experts in rocketry at the close of World War II immediately to find convenient accommodation with new employers, the Soviet Union or the West, depending upon into which sphere of influence the arbitrary postwar border accidentally placed their homes. Overburdening mankind, as does the scientist with the costs and the side effects of his new discoveries, the easy challenges such as man's inventions to search the heavens and to prolong or destroy life, and in return obtaining a comfortable, privileged living is intellectual Epicureanism. Little wonder this was the only heresy Dante found in the lower rungs of hell.

I would like to conclude this toughest chapter yet with a digression and a compliment. The digression is the meaning of the word *sacrament*. It is not a Greek word. The New Testament was written in Greek, but Greek had no word for the sacramental concept. It is from a Latin word that had two meanings. The second meaning was "the initiation rite for an army recruit." The first meaning fascinates me. It was the amount of money each civil litigant had to put up out of his own pocket to have the courts hear his case. The winner received back what he had put up. The loser's *sacramentum* was given to the gods for religious purposes.

The compliment is given to the Roman hierarchy. Please look at the work priests do. Priests have to be theologians to study about God, teachers to teach about God, evangelists to tell of the love of God, and apostles to believe that their calling is God's will for them. In addition, in order to serve this institution they cannot be burdened with service to the other two necessary institutions. Consequently, they voluntarily forgo having a family of their own or entering politics. Although other branches of the church are also to be complimented, there is no doubt that Rome is second to none in bringing the good news of the gospel to entire continents. I rely upon this missionary activity, combined with the active support of the wise and the good from all parts of the world, to achieve our goal of 100 percent worldwide membership in a universal voluntary community. What today are called sectarian differences I envision as being overcome by the elimination of Rome's compulsions and the grant of much local autonomy in the form and content of worship.

Chapter VII
On Righteousness

This chapter, coming as it does between that devoted to the voluntary community and that devoted to the mandatory community, is transitional. It prepares you for the complete change of standards that appear in the next chapter.

In pleading for an understanding audience in one of his *Federalist Papers,* James Madison, a southern aristocrat, initiates a problem politely: "When the Almighty himself condescends to address mankind in their own language, his meaning, luminous as it may be, is rendered dim and doubtful by the cloudy medium through which it is communicated." Now I have to take this thought one step further. As God chooses to speak to man using the words of man, then I, to make my point, may use a word of man to try to describe God, and in my so doing you will notice that despite my comment in the first chapter, I am extremely hung up on three words: *love, law,* and *righteousness.*

God is love is the expression currently in vogue, so let us talk about love. I stumbled upon a fresh insight into the meaning of the word *love* two years ago. It brought me such pleasure that even though it is a long story, I shall share it with you in all its detail. I was trying to understand the grammatical concept of a prefix. As you know, a prefix is a word or a portion of a word, usually a preposition or an adverb, often of foreign origin, placed before a word so as to modify or change the meaning of the word. Sometimes, according to one dictionary, the meaning of the prefix becomes lost in the meaning of the base word, but its impact remains apparent. In the word *downtown* the adverb prefix *down* is not lost, because in a country such as ours, where the first towns were seaports, the main part of town down at the port, called the downtown, was down from the surrounding land. But the prefix derived from the Greek word meaning "down" in the sense of "thrown down" is often lost in the word itself, though its impact remains apparent. This Greek prefix is *kata* when the base word starts with a consonant and *kath* when the base word starts with a vowel. As there was no *k* in Latin except in a few proper names, like Kalends, *c* supplants *k* in English. Thus *cata* before the Greek word *pallein,* which means "to brandish," becomes *catapult,* meaning "to hurl down." *Cata* before *cumba,* which means "boat that carries the dead," becomes *catacomb,* a subterranean burial place. *Cath* before *hedra,* which means "seat," becomes *cathedral,* where the bishop sits down. *Cata* before *strephein,* which means "to turn," becomes *catastrophe,* meaning "to turn down," hence, "to overturn." *Cata* before *kluzein,* which means "to wash," becomes *cataclysm,* meaning "to wash down like a flood." *Cata* before *rassein,* which means "to strike," becomes *cataract,* meaning a waterfall or eye growth. *Cata* before *luein,* which means "to loosen," becomes *catalyst,* a substance that dissolves other substances. *Cath* before *hodus,* which means "way," becomes *cathode,* an electrical conductor, because electric current was once believed to flow from east to west, the down way, as the sun goes down in the west. *Cata* before *rhein,* which means "to flow," becomes *catarrh,* a mucous inflammation. *Cath* before *hienai,* which means "to send," becomes *catheter,* the tube sent down into a body channel. *Cata* before *legein,* which means "to gather," becomes *catalogue,* where gathering or listings of things are put down on paper. *Cata* before *agora,* which means "assembly," becomes *category,* which originally was a grouping of those put down or accused in the public gatherings. *Cata* before *ekhein,* which means "to sound," becomes *catechism,* the earliest oral teachings put down in question and answer form. *Cata* before *holus,* which means "whole," becomes *catholic,* the whole thing put down pat, as in this catholic book. *Catharsis,* however, in the few dictionaries I have checked, merely comes, without breakdown, from the Greek word *katharos,* which means "pure," from which comes *Katharine* or, more commonly, *Catherine.* Yet some dictionaries say the origin of *Catherine* is obscure or unknown, which immediately prompts me to become, first, suspicious and, then, imaginative, like the pontificator at the dinner party. So here we go again.

The Greeks were thinkers who liked to put their thinkings into compartments. Thus man had a body, mind, and soul. Thus there were three words for love: *eros* for bodily love, *philos* for mental love, and *agape* for spiritual love. Voilà! *Cath* before *eros* becomes *Catherine.* How the meaning of the prefix has been lost in the meaning of the word, but how effective its impact. Down, serpent! Little wonder that biblical translators, in choosing a word for the greatest Christian virtue, gave up on the English word *love* and substituted the word *charity,* which comes from the Latin word for love, *caritas,* a substitution whose secondary effects can be seen to this day in the minds of those who believe a good name in the community can be bought by the doing of good works. The church, admittedly, has never lost sight of St. Paul's use of the word *agape*. She has always appreciated the concept of spiritual love. I find such love best understood by the poet in his verse "the gift without the giver is bare," and I see such love present whenever two or more are talking or working together through the grace and power of the holy spirit.

But *love,* whether in the form of good works, good speakings, or good thoughts, is not a strong enough word by itself to describe God. At their worst, good works risk one's casting his pearls to swine and good speakings and good thoughts risk one's stagnating on the road to hell, paved as it is with good intentions. I know the parlor folk dislike my thus viewing good things at their worst, so I offer this serpentine observation. Good people often say, "I believe in God but forget the church." It's enough just to call God the idea of loving and the idea of helping those who suffer. Beware lest they accept your love and good works, which cannot harm their smugness. Test them by asking if they would be willing just to call God the idea of righteousness. Their fear of your righteousness will cause them to show you a fair pair of heels. Hence my word to describe God has to be broad enough to include God's judgment.

In order to include the feeling of judgment, should we say God is law? Many have done so and still do. Today many more act as though God were the law without realizing it. Who among us does not believe in justice under law? Who does not believe the law is necessary to show the difference between right and wrong? In our pluralistic democratic society, the law is the only power superior to that of man, the only power to which man is subordinate other than nature, and the power that ties all of us together. Religion, as I understand it, concerns itself with the relationship between God and mankind and, as its etymology suggests, contemplates the binding back of mankind to God after Adam's fall. If so, the law, the tie that binds us, is our religion today. Some years ago, a false prophet, a U.S. senator from Philadelphia, gave this religion its purest expression when, in an article in the *Atlantic Monthly,* he exhorted the people to use the full force of government to achieve social justice. Thus far I have said nothing compelling to dramatize the rottenness of the law, so let me take three approaches: first, a definitional reductio ad absurdum; secondly, a contemplation of the meaning of the death of Jesus; and lastly, an attempt to explain the concept to children.

First Approach

In any fair society laws should govern all uniformly. Laws should be public laws. There should not be private laws favoring individuals. In other words, no one should be privileged, because privilege comes from *privus* and *legis* (*lex*) and means single law. No one should benefit from private laws, and so everyone should be un-private-lawed, unprivileged. Yet the thrust of our legal system today is to help the underprivileged, presumably by having everyone become privileged with private laws for everyone, several hundred million of them. Not only is this thrust logically absurd, but also its practical effect is that of selective enforcement and application of the law. Those who are moneyed can hire shrewd and enterprising attorneys, so the bright and moneyed few live off the industrious and uninformed and maintain society's uneasy equilibrium by tossing the poor their privileged crumbs.

Second Approach

Yesterday I came across a passage in Scripture that had never been brought to my attention, presumably because the footnote said its meaning was unknown. [By now you are aware of the enjoyment I take in pontificating in this type of situation.] After the childhood of Jesus, he is introduced to us by John the Baptist, who, instead of looking for a great leader in the future, goes about preaching; "Repent, for the kingdom of God is at hand," a phrase that Jesus himself then begins to use. In the verse of unknown meaning Jesus says later in his ministry to an impatient John; "And from the days of John the Baptist until now the kingdom of heaven suffereth violence and the violent take it by force" (Matthew 11:12). This verse gives me no problem. Let us see why. My book is an attempt to find the best form of government. It is not an exercise in theology. Its concern with Jesus is limited to trying to understand the kind of kingdom he was espousing, especially if it were to take the form of a government for this world. Jesus never gave any specifics about the earthly kingdom he said was at hand, but his actions during the last week of his earthly life are available for those who have eyes to read, minds to evaluate hearsay, and, hopefully, the grace of God to understand. What caused the death of Jesus? What was the purpose of his death? The harmless dovelike answer of the resurrection is irrelevant to my discussion. The answer of the wise serpent is: Jesus died to show the world that God's law killed God. Let us analyze the serpent's response.

What happened during that last week? On Sunday the people proclaimed Jesus king. That was followed by his whipping the money changers out of the temple.

Thursday night he took on Judas. Judas had become far more impatient than John the Baptist had ever been. Judas had followed Jesus believing him to be the long-promised good, great, and forceful king. Jesus had done nothing to deny this expectation. Judas felt betrayed. So Jesus struck first. He predicted that Judas would betray him and told Judas to act quickly. Later that very night the soldiers apprehended Jesus and Jesus rebuked the disciple who used his sword in at attempt to thwart the arrest. The next day Jesus was crucified. Earlier that last day Pilate had asked, "What has this man done?"

Jesus was considered a criminal by the church leaders whose theocratic duty it was to interpret and enforce the laws of God. At the very beginning of Jesus's three-year ministry he had been accused of breaking the "blue laws" by working on Sunday. He had been healing people on that day. The legal interpretation involved was that healing is work, as any doctor would agree. By the end of his ministry Jesus had so berated and ridiculed the priestly rulers that I doubt anyone could use such language today and get off a contempt rap.

But all Jesus had really done was show that the kingdom had suffered violence in his lifetime from the hands of the violent. Translated into the idiom of our day, this is to say: government is maintained violently through wars abroad and tear gas at home and maintained even in time of peace through the ever-present threat of violence: obey the laws or be jailed. Jesus' crime was to point out that mandatory government is not the answer, even when in the hands of the good people, the priests who execute the laws of God. Jesus showed that the right form of kingdom can be worked for among us now, but the process requires absolute rejection of mandatory government. Government can do no good, only what is necessary. When government purported to do more, God's all-embracing law stifled the spirit of God himself even unto death.

So what Jesus did was redefine the kingdom. No longer would the search be for a wise and just ruler, for no matter how wise and just he is, his rule is predicated on violence and the threat of violence. Insofar as the kingdom is concerned, the meaning of the death of Jesus is that we must search for a government where violence is not allowed in its administration. The word *allow* is proper current usage for this archaic meaning of the word *suffer.*

You ask, Is there really any meaningful difference between what is good and what is necessary in speaking of the functions of government? On the meaningfulness of this difference rests all the value this book may have, so let us proceed pedantically. *Good* is a positive concept. *Necessary* waffles. It has a feeling of inevitability, as in the expression *the necessary,* a backwoods term for the outhouse. I like to think of *necessary* as composed of the Latin words *nec* and *esse* and as representing the denial of the spirit, the denial of the *esse,* the same *esse* about which medieval scholars wrote volumes for centuries until finally a great poet put it simply: "To be or not to be, that is the question." Present-day existentialists continue to struggle with this question. Even though the dictionary says *necessary* comes from *nec* (not) and *cessi* (to go away) and means "inevitable, unavoidable, or not voluntary," note that something that won't go away, that is, something that is "to be" in the sense of being destined to happen, smacks more of fate, especially of the Roman goddess's cutting the thread of one's life, than of the spirit, the *esse,* and the option that God has given man "to be." So *necessity,* in all its dirty expediency, is the principle we will be dealing with in the next chapter.

Third Approach

Finally, there follows a letter I wrote to my two sons when they had reached puberty:

I had a dream for my life, a dream that I failed to help make come true, although I tried and, in trying, the dream brought me much peace. It is such a wonderful dream that I pass it on to you.

My dream is that someday people will be so good and so bright that they will always do the right thing of their own free will without having to be made to do it by any force or any law.

A few of the great minds in history have had similar thoughts. The philosophers call the concept philosophical anarchy. The way you understand philosophical anarchy is, first, to think of the word *anarchy. Anarchy* comes from two Greek words meaning "no" and "government." We believe we must have government or the bad people might destroy us. Others believe government is also necessary to enable things to get done that otherwise might not get done. Next you think about government with its law and authority. If you study history carefully, you will see how governments often bring more problems than they solve and you will see why the best government is that which governs least. Finally, you think of a world where the people are so bright and so good that government is unnecessary.

The key to the understanding of my dream is the law. The law is very good to study, to train your mind, to know about, and to obey. The law is a fine way to make a living by practicing it as a lawyer. The law is a far better way for government to keep order than war is. But the law is an awful waste of time, which could much better be spent on the beautiful things in life, and the law is the worst thing in the world to believe in. My explanation of the following diagram shows why:

GOOD ME BAD

My life has been spent trying to make enough to bring up a family, but I have always been squeezed into financial inability by the good people and the bad people. The good people are those who believe in God and who believe his justice and mercy require society to provide all people with all the necessities of life that they do not have. This requires the working people, including me, to pay very large taxes. The bad people are those who are able to but do not pay their share of taxes. Any bright person, if he spends enough time at it, can find a way not to pay much tax. The more bad people who do not pay their share of taxes, the greater the taxes I must pay. And the saddest fact is that more often than not the same people are often both the good ones and the bad ones. For when the good people see how much taxes it takes to give all the people all the things that their God in his justice and mercy require of them, they use every brain in their head to avoid paying such large taxes in order to keep enough money to be able very comfortably to take care of their families, salving their consciences with the thought that everybody cheats on taxes. What a vicious situation!

Now let us return to my dream. If the good people did not try to force other people to be good—if the good people just tried to be good themselves—if the good people let me be free to make up my own mind to help other people—if the good people would set a good example for me and be a good witness for me—boys, do you begin to recognize Jesus Christ in my dream? Do you now begin to see as he saw how the good people fail to understand the way of God? This is why Jesus is the way and the truth and why he will make you free. Please do not give up this wonderful tradition lightly.

* * * * *

Here I must insert a side-bar expansion of my above elliptic statement that the good people avoid paying taxes by cheating. Their approach is far more sophisticated. They delegate their tax work to hired accountants to avoid the bother, making no attempt and having no desire to understand any of it at all. For their part, the accountants realize their fees increase with their clients' tax savings, and understood by both accountant and client is the realization that, in view of the few returns the Internal Revenue Service audits, the risk-benefit test justifies taking aggressive tax positions that may not withstand challenge.

All of which brings us to the conclusion of this transitional chapter. *Love* is too weak a word to describe the fullness of God, especially as it does not encompass any concept of God's justice or judgment. *Law* is too harsh and negative a word to describe the fullness of God, especially as the law embraces no concept of God's love and, indeed, limits God's spirit. Laws and more laws—no-nos—leave us feeling like children endlessly nagged with no opening to let our spirit become free without breaking the laws. Yet only by voluntary following the spirit without breaking the law can we expect to flourish in the land that floweth with milk and honey. Yes, God is more than love and more than law. God is what is right. His way is the right way. So I am left with the word *righteousness* as the best word to use to try to describe God. *Righteousness* embraces both love and law. The right way is God's way of love. The right law is God's law, but without sanctions known to man.

I have always found St. Paul to be tough reading and I have always considered him to be something of a public relations or Madison Avenue type, huckstering Jesus, but having finished my struggle with this chapter I was pleased to come upon his verse in Philippians 3:9: ". . . not having a righteousness of mine own, based on law, but that which is through faith in Christ, the righteousness from God that depends on faith."

Chapter VIII
A Mandatory Community

The expression *mandatory community* is a euphuism for *government*. I use the expression as a contrast to the voluntary community that I am trying to strengthen. Although I dislike the expression *mandatory community,* I also use it because the old English use of words from the same root as *mandatory*'s root dramatizes the ease with which the unwary may slip from the voluntary community, to which we say yes, to the mandatory community, to which we say yes reluctantly because it is necessary now. Here follows the story that illustrates this point. I caution you will find the beginning of this chapter anecdotal and disconnected, a stream of consciousness pushing me relentlessly along a course I would rather not follow, as is ever the case when necessity forces the way.

The last full day of Jesus' life is called Maundy Thursday because that evening after his last supper with his apostles he gave them the new commandment that they love one another. *Maundy* is from the Latin *mando,* which means "put in hand, deliver over, or order." Maundy moneys, however, were alms that the kings of England used to give the poor on that day. To which you say, "So what?" Now I am going to tell a story so that you may see and remember the point.

Fifi was the pride of all France, beautiful and expensive. The lads at Saint-Cyr, as not one of them could afford her price, held a lottery, each contributing one sou. After the bargain had been consummated, Fifi asked the winner where he had got the money and upon learning was very touched. In an impassioned speech she exclaimed, "Never let it be said that Fifi ever took anything from a cadet of the academy that is the pride of all France!" Whereupon she gave him back his sou.

Other people's money, that is what the world is all about, and other people's principles. Jesus may command me, but I resent commands from others: kings, clerics, or bureaucrats in both establishments, because they tax me and spend my money for their purposes and if they will do it to my money they will try to do it to me.

Professor George Knowles Gardner began his opening lecture in his class on the Law of Contracts something like this: "Gentlemen, there are only three ways by which man has been able to get along with his fellowman: by habit, by war, and by the Law of Contracts." (I admire one who glories in his work, although I never took any glory in the Law of Contracts.) Continuing, he said, "When something unforeseen comes along, habit can not handle it, so you have war unless there is an enforceable contract." I tell this story because I suspect many of you may think I overreact to being pushed around. These are those readers who, if they should take the time to think about it, have made a convenient accommodation with their community and, therefore, suffer being pushed around gladly out of force of habit, but when the accommodation and the law are taken away from them, they are the first to squeal, as we shall shortly see.

In the early sixties Professor Carl Friedrich was touring the luncheon circuit giving a five-minute address that I remember somewhat as follows:

There is, he said, a dangerous trend toward anarchy in the world today caused by three factors:

1. The rising expectations of the people for all the things that their governments have promised but, of course, been unable to produce have left people all over the world disillusioned and apathetic.
2. The classical method for the commencement of war whereby a nation gives an ultimatum to its enemy nation has gone out of fashion and is being replaced by guerrilla and terrorist tactics.
3. Just as before the three revolutions (American, 1776; French, 1787; and Russian, 1917) people were questioning the divine right of kings to rule them, a right that Europe had recognized since 313, when Constantine established Christianity as the state religion, so today people are questioning the divine right of the ballot box, which allows a majority, or often even less, to rule them.

Little wonder that just last week the president of the United States weakly squealed that if Libya does not cease state-sponsored terrorism we shall have to do something and followed up the threat with the bombing of Libya. The professors would not have been surprised. The habitual had changed so that only two options were left. But for me only one option is left. Just as in an earlier chapter I said I could not be happy as long as there was one unhappy person in the world, so I cannot consider war as an instrument of policy, as it involves the ultimate unhappiness, the death of youth. Hence necessity now compels me to promulgate a law of contracts for the entire world. You may not like this promulgation any more than the burly Michigan backwoodsman liked the lawyer who took away from him his home where he had lived from childhood under deed the court found defective despite the intervening years. The woodsman commented, "I'd have had more respect for him if he had punched me."

By these stories I have tried to prepare you for our present undertaking. It will be an exercise in raw wisdom in its most serpentine form. There will be nothing righteous about it. Jesus has nothing whatsoever to do with it. You will remember that Jesus knocked institutions, drove the money changers out of the temple, and cursed the avaricious Pharisees (church leaders), saying they not only cheated on God but also did not even have the worldly brains to use their money to buy friends. Jesus was trying to purify the temple, as he knew the house of God was the only institution that could help the people. When it came to government he said nothing, as though in Paretan silence to indicate contempt. The Christian who boasts that he is in the world but not of it is a fool unless he immediately adds that he is a repentant sinner. You ask, If Christians as Christians, and especially the church, cannot take part in a mandatory community, by what dispensation do I have the boldness now to try to create one? I answer, By poetic license allowed one who is blank in verse but hopefully not blank in thought. If the excommunicated Dante could spend the longest day I have ever read about in hell telling about its infirmities in order to defend the faith, why can not I now outline a most sordid steel-trapped mandatory community, workable, but so obnoxious that all will look forward to its withering away upon the coming of the kingdom? Before doing so, however, I shall first set forth the overall standards I shall follow.

All of my life I have been on the alert for a philosophy of life that, without involving any divine concept, tied itself to some high standard. The only one I ever found that captured my imagination, though only for a fleeting moment, was George Santayana's. His conclusion was that the highest accomplishment of which man is capable is to live honorably. Santayana's "honor" probably had its origins in old Rome, where admittedly it received support from the gods. You may remember those sonorous Latin expressions of honor: "We who are about to die salute you," is what the soldiers exclaimed upon being presented to the Roman Senate before leaving for war. "There is nothing more honorable than to die for the fatherland," is the sentiment their salutation reflected. Even Hamilton, whose writings in the *Federalist Papers* gave our constitution its most incisive intellectual support, in weaker moments appealed to patriotism and philanthropy as well as to reason. I say "weaker" remembering the earlier chapter in which I wanted to be like the tiger. These honorable sentiments are not tiger talk. They are money talk, the talk of those who know they need the group for protection and/or plunder.

Accordingly, it is going to be difficult to find a star from which to hang this chapter. Lawyers often use a trite ploy when representing a client in negotiations where the other side appears to be in the right, saying; "Gentlemen, we each must have the courage to rise above our principle and look to our interest, or both of us will lose." You will remember we left our principles in the last chapter with the understanding this chapter could not have any, so interest will be the test, but whose interest? If Jeremy Bentham can say government should concern itself with the greatest good for the greatest number, I can say it should concern itself with the least necessary for the greatest number.

You ask, Do you really mean that your government is going to be unprincipled? Touché! Of course not, so here is my next story. A fine Philadelphia lawyer was giving a brilliant lecture to a large group of extremely knowledgeable lawyers on the complicated business-judgment rule applicable to directors and officers of business corporations. In commenting upon the many references in the applicable statutes to a requirement that these individuals act in good faith he asked, "What is good faith?" While my mind was leaving things legal and coming up with the church's answer, *sole fide,* the only faith that one lives by faith alone, he answered his own question: "No one knows what good faith is. It cannot be defined. All it means, I guess, is absence of bad faith, and everyone knows what bad faith is." Logically I am not sure that I do, but I admit that my government must be a good-faith government and must pass the smell test.

I would prefer to outline a model government for a theoretical little island in the South Pacific. Then I would be able to present the concepts more logically and without emotion. I start with a government whose membership embraces the entire world, however, because the times demand that I do so. Look at the mess the world is in today. Look at how our best minds are merely band-aiding the problems without taking, or perhaps without having, the time to devote themselves to the cure. We have a trillion-dollar arms race between the two most powerful nations. Throughout history periods of peace have usually been marked either by the domination of one powerful nation ruling the then known world or by several nations maintaining a precarious balance of power. At some point this balance is upset when one of these nations or an outside nation becomes dominant not usually because it has the superior culture, but rather because it has acquired the latest sophistication in weaponry, whether crossbow, gunpowder, armored battleship, armored tank, atomic bomb, or whatever comes next. *Jane's* says the Soviet's space program dwarfs ours today so the bomb of time is ticking. We have seen the leaders of these two powers waste millions in trying futilely to negotiate treaties with respect to nonverifiable matters, as both sides are not sure whether unleashing their lethal weapons is in their best interest yet. Neither side, of course, states this position so bluntly. If and when the time comes, the euphuistic justification will be that the use of the weapons was necessary to the national defense and, more probably, to the survival of its peoples. Neither side is willing to remember that treaties, even if agreed upon, are an ineffective solution, because when they are broken, war is the only effective response. Both sides, from unwillingness to give up any sovereignty, from unwillingness to see themselves diminished, merely toy with today's first steps toward mandatory international institutions whose fainéance reminds one of the Articles of Confederation. The situation is so bad that responsible leaders of the church in our country are calling for unilateral disarmament even though they have no business usurping the political functions that our political leaders and our citizenry have abdicated. What is even more frightening is that daily the lifelines of the several nations become increasingly intertwined with the ever-increasing threat that a powerful nation's lifeline may accidentally be cut and the mythological scales that hold the world power in balance may disappear. These lifelines affect all interrelationships of nations, economic, financial, legal, scientific, as well as political. Only last month an accident at an energy-producing plant in one country brought fear and fact of deadly radiation to surrounding countries. Regularly, unidentified terrorists disrupt these lifelines and avoid the posses merely by boarding an airplane. I can remember from the movies the good old days when they had at least to ride all night on horseback under hot pursuit over rugged terrain to get to the border. Today even the movies are hard pressed to keep up with the gross events of real life. So let's get on with the task of immediately creating a world government. If you laughed at my vision of philosophical anarchy in earlier chapters, then for the sake of your personal intellectual integrity take seriously the increasing no-holds-barred anarchy of our world. Leave your getting and spending for long enough to join the task force. For starters I will now have a go at a constitution for the world.

To be consistent with concepts expressed in prior chapters, ideally any mandatory world community should have a membership consisting of the people of the world, an organization in the nature of a democracy, and the purpose of fulfilling the physical and mental needs of all its members to the extent that families and voluntary and local mandatory communities fail in their duty to fill such needs. Realistically, however, any world government at this time, as it is so urgently needed, must have, at least initially, a far more limited purpose, namely, the maintenance of peace between nations and the abolition of national armed forces, in order for it to find acceptance by the several nations. With such a limited purpose we next focus on what form of organization and membership will be most acceptable and still pass the smell test.

The wheel that comes to mind is the U.S. Constitution. Jefferson boasted, and probably correctly, that ours was the first written constitution in history, the first time man had ever written down the nature of his government, its function, and its limits, the first government that derived its powers from the people, and hence the first self-government. Even today, two hundred years later, I suspect most people would agree with Churchill's accurately weighed description of it: the worst form of government except for every other form the world has ever seen.

Right at the threshold, however, I have to make a major change for my world constitution. The ultimate source of power cannot reside in the people, as it does in our constitution. At the beginning, at least, such power must reside in the member nations. As we must have a strong world government, strong enough to harness the competing energies of the superpowers in their fantastic and costly imagination for defensive weaponry, the trick will be to keep the people out of it except to the extent necessary. When you have too many people involved you never get anything done. As a matter of fact, in 1787 people were directly involved in the U.S. Constitution only in two ways: (1) power was stated abstractly as being derived from the people; and (2) representation in the House of Representatives resulted from popular vote of free persons . . . and three-fifths of other persons, but the other persons had no franchise for over seventy-five years and no equal vote (the one man, one vote concept) for over seventy-five years more. Therefore, I propose the world government derive its power from the nations, representation of the nations be based upon something other than population, and nations, not people, have the franchise. Lest I be accused of turning back the clock of history on the concept of self-government, I now support my proposals with theoretical and practical reasons.

As a tiger I have always been a member of the smallest minority, a minority of one. As such, the right to vote, the right that provides my liberty and allows peaceful change, has meant relatively little to me. Throughout my working life Caesar has confiscated the cream from my endeavors, in recent years over 50 percent of my earnings, mostly for programs in which I do not believe. I, who am without unearned income and unwilling to play the deduction game and fight Caesar on his own level, have been diminished. So as daily my personal lifeline becomes increasingly intertwined with those of so many others, I am immediately intimidated whenever I see any group gathering. Accidentally or intentionally, they could unplug my lifeline. I see only three options open to me when a group uses their votes to push me around: (1) join them, although this often may not be an option; (2) join another group and push back, or (3) slowly be destroyed. Mandatory government never brings out the best in anyone, including me. Understandably, the weak group together to defend themselves against the strong, but in an imperfect world, which offers at best only an imperfect security, the defense the weak group needs, as they in their togetherness grow stronger, can easily and unwittingly cross the line of what is a proper defense and result in the destruction of other groups and especially of other individuals. Today for the first time I see how England's common-law judges were struggling with this same problem at the beginning of the trade-union movement. You may remember their ridiculous definition for the crime of conspiracy that was, in part: "any gathering of employees is unlawful when they are acting in concert to perform that which for an individual to perform would be a lawful act." My conclusion is that the vote is a divisive but necessary concept used by factions and parties, that I properly am alarmed whenever people talk in terms of groups that embrace either less than or more than the entire membership of the particular mandatory institution out of which the talk emanates, and that it is necessary for me to point out this alarm whenever it impedes the immediate creation of a world government.

With respect to the one man, one vote concept, I think it may be a sound concept for a New England town-meeting form of democratic government in a small community. It certainly is a necessary concept for our country today, although we are still a long way from having digested it. Clearly, however, it is a premature concept for my world government when one realizes that over 75 percent of the world's people, now estimated to number over 5 billion, live in Latin America, Africa, and Asia (excluding the USSR and Japan), continents abounding in poverty and famine.

Today any world government to be successful has to derive its powers from the several nations working together. To this end it is necessary that each nation try not to interfere in the domestic matters of another, although when any such domestic matter jeopardizes the peace of the world it then becomes an international problem. If there still remain readers who, unwilling to accept the conclusions in my prior chapters, continue to believe governments can do good and having people speak out for such good through the ballot box is the way to bring this about, then they will understand this is another reason why I must disenfranchise them in my world government, as our country and Russia must work together. This can never occur as long as we insist on telling them how rotten they are. Let those whose conscience compels them to tell any other nation how to handle its domestic affairs do so as missionaries within the missionary's framework of a voluntary institution and not as politicians within a mandatory framework. Whenever religious leaders try to wear two hats, miter and crown, we witness a most primitive violation of the doctrine of the separation of church and state. As one cannot be a missionary to a nation that refuses entry, I visualize in the early years after the adoption of the world constitution an amendment that establishes rules with respect to immigration, including permanent and temporary exit from and/or entry into member nations.

In any event, I have now finished drafting my world constitution, which may be found in the appendix. For several reasons I make no attempt to integrate my discussion of it that follows with the constitution itself appearing in the appendix. These reasons are:

1. *Readability.* Comments should be readable. Written constitutions are legal documents and can have no loopholes. I do not care how many statutes are enacted requiring legal documents like insurance contracts to be written in everyday language; the precision required in a legal document prevents it from being composed of short declaratory sentences. For this reason I do not clutter up my ideological comments with references to the appendix.
2. *Practicality.* In the creation of any legal document that is to serve two or more equal parties, after they all accept underlining concepts, the only way to proceed is by negotiating out of drafts of the document. One party submits a complete draft of what he would be willing to accept. Then the others ask for specific changes by submitting redrafts changing unacceptable portions. If recalcitrant parties merely voice objections or write comments or memoranda the job never gets done. The reason for this is that in comments and simple declaratory sentences only the flavor of the meaning is important, whereas in legal documents the actual

meaning applicable to all situations depends upon subtle nuances arising from the use, placement, and repetition of words. Dignifying the unnegotiated appendix at this point would be both premature and a waste of time.

3. *Laziness*. Remember, I am writing this book to be joyful. It is a cost-free medical attendant for my old age. [Would you believe *therapeutic* means "medical attendant" in old Greek?] The book loses its therapeutic value if I take myself too seriously or attempt to be scholarly. On the other hand, as all of my life I have always criticized the pet programs of others and always been asked what would I do, I could not write about a better world without including the first written world constitution. The appendix, if it serves no other purpose, will provide a good checklist for those who eventually have the task of writing or negotiating such a document.

I shall now comment upon my world constitution article by article. These comments include the major changes and additions I have made to the U.S. Constitution, whose format and many of whose provisions I have kept, often verbatim.

First, referring to the preamble, for reasons I have already indicated, the nations of the world and not its peoples are the ones who are forming this government. I am not unmindful, in thus empowering nations rather than people, that the founding fathers believed the Articles of Confederation were weak, in part because they represented a confederation of sovereign states and as such in the event of irresoluble disputes war was the only solution, whereas a constitution of the people enables resolution of all disputes through the courts and the punishment of individual wrongdoers. Accordingly, in limited instances, I have subjected miscreants to world criminal courts, especially those who, charged with the duty of carrying out the functions of the world government, break their oath to support and defend the world constitution.

I am also not unmindful that even after we had the strong U.S. Constitution the doctrine of states' rights nearly destroyed the union. Despite this, I am intentionally keeping my world government weak in many areas. I do not want a supergovernment. In this country it is gross that we already are governed on three levels: local, state, and national. If for any reason my world constitution should prove to be too weak to be effective, it can always be amended, just as the colonists had to revise the Articles of Confederation. In the meantime the nations of the world will have had the much needed experience of having tried to govern together.

Next, before referring to the numbered articles, please note preliminarily that as in the U.S. Constitution, power has been divided among branches or distinct departments of the government: legislative, to make laws as limited by a written constitution adopted at the inception of the government; executive, to enforce the laws; and judicial, to interpret them. In addition, a system of checks and balances has been used in an attempt to thwart the visionary and the designing without on the one hand weakening the executive or on the other hand complicating the structure, as a complicated structure customarily results in the shrewd and enterprising living off the workers.

Let us now refer to article 1, titled "The Legislative Department." My first consideration was to avoid a clumsy organization. The number of legislators should be manageable. Too few may result in cabals who lose sight of their representations and of their oaths to uphold the constitution; too many, being "unmanageable" and thus manageable only by gods, may result in dictators who think of themselves as demigods. I think I could work best with about 100 legislators, but no more than that. Next then is how do we apportion the 100 seats among the membership in an institution that may consist of over 100 nations? Easily discarded is any thought of one seat having greater voting power than another, as this concept is too complicated. Also discardable is any thought of each nation having one seat, as this concept is unfair. Left is the thought of each seat representing one-hundredth of the world's something or other.

Should the legislative seats be allotted based on the populations of the member nations? We have already decided that the world government is to derive its powers from the member nations and that, at least, at first it will not interfere in the domestic matters of the member nations. This means that the member nations will fill their allotted seats in any way they see fit and not necessarily by popular vote. It follows, therefore, that seats should not be awarded based upon population. For nations to be entitled to representation based upon the number of their people, some or all of whom were not enfranchised, would be as incongruous as it was to let the southern states in 1787 include in their population base for representation three for every five of their people who did not have the right to vote. Moreover, in view of the very limited purpose of my world constitution, which deals in no way with social welfare, its structure must be at least population-neutral, that is, it cannot encourage the Mussolinis of the world to give baby bonuses to increase their representation nor can it discourage China's one-baby-per-family program. A requirement that a nation have sovereignty over a hundredth of the land area of the earth to be entitled to a seat in the world congress would also not be an appropriate solution, as Japan would immediately inform you. What would be appropriate? Well, why do you really need a government? What is the bare necessity for a government? Protection is the answer, and for protection one should pay protection money. Even bad people like the Mafia cannot be stupid and survive; they understand this concept. Next, then, is what does any nation have to protect? "Its sacred honor?" you ask to needle me; to which I reply that in my accounting rules for totaling the assets (the protectables) of a nation, intangibles, such as sacred honor and goodwill, shall not be included.

The statement of assets shall include all tangible assets, real and personal, and all intangible assets of a financial nature. Shaking your head, you interrupt: "You idiot, you are providing everlasting annuities for lawyers, accountants, and appraisers. How do you define intangible financial assets? How do you value such assets, or for that matter, how do you value land? People, too, are to be protected. Are they to have no value?"

In reply, with reference to what should be included in financial assets, modern multinational corporations are able to prepare such statements so that there is no reason why a nation should not also be able to, following a simple set of guidelines. The key here is expressly to provide that assets cannot be offset by debts of any nature, as the assets require protection regardless of the amount of the national debt. A cute way to circumvent this expressed prohibition would be for a nation to sell an asset to another nation under an agreement to repurchase it and under provisions that require the selling nation to be responsible for its protection. We shall see shortly that any such circumventions will be both self-defeating and unnecessary.

The troublesome problem, of course, is valuation, especially as it involves two assets that have to be protected yet are not capable of evaluation by man, namely, land and people. This problem cannot be solved, so now we must revert to serpentine wisdom. The straightforward approach to any difficult valuation problem is to consult an appraiser. If one has such a problem and is dealing in the marketplace, one should hire as many excellent appraisers for his side as the subject matter justifies. But if one is trying to create a simple, good-faith government he is dealing not with the morals of the marketplace, but with "a punctilio of an honor the most sensitive," and in this situation appraisers are worthless. In real estate a professional title often given appraisers is M.A.I. I never can remember the meaning of these letters, as we always said they meant: "Made As Indicated." Remember the three types of witnesses: liars, damn liars, and expert witnesses. Is there any other group who could possibly help us? Not actuaries, as they always have a problem for every solution. Nor politicians, as they always confuse what they cannot clarify. But lawyers can help, as they are paid to provide solutions for every problem, including insolvable ones. Let us see how this lawyer solves the insolvable valuation problem, remembering Jesus pitied lawyers and found them to be miserable because they add to man's problems without participating in them.

My first suggestion is to avoid the valuation problem by giving it to somebody else. My second suggestion is to neutralize its impact by having high valuations carry correspondingly high insurance premiums and by having low valuations that do not meet the smell test jeopardize the receipt by the nations submitting such low valuations of proper protection. My support for this second suggestion is found in our 1787 constitution that apportioned representation in the House of Representatives among the states on the same basis as was the federal tax burden apportioned. Accordingly, the world government will accept without question the unaudited, uncertified statement of assets furnished by each nation at the beginning and at every eighth year reapportionment thereafter, bill each nation its share of the annual budget based upon such valuation, and grant each nation its share of seats in the legislature in the ratio that the amount assessed and paid bears to the total budget. Military personnel to meet the recruiting needs of the world government will be furnished by the nations in fulfillment of quotas, which will be calculated on the same basis as assessments.

The question of what person shall fill each seat in the congress and for what term will be left to the discretion of the participating nation whose contributions entitle it to the seat. As this is a government of nations, each nation must be able to control its voice in the congress. Although long terms would be desirable, as they tend to improve competence and responsibility, controlling is the fact that the holder of the seat must be responsible at all times to the nation he represents. It is contemplated, therefore, that on the one hand the several nations will appoint their best representatives, in the hope of their attaining the benefits of seniority on the congressional committees, and on the other hand the representatives may resign when called upon by their nations to vote contrary to their own perception, especially when such a vote might be held to be admissible in the world criminal courts as evidence of their aiding their nations in the commission of some act of treason against the world government.

As previously indicated, membership in the congress is bought by payment of assessments based upon declared assets. To those of you who are as tired as I am with the inordinate amount of time and money wasted on our country's election procedures, I ask, Have I not created an election that can be bought without waste of time or expense of effort in electioneering, but at a price no nation can afford? If so, the solution seems obvious. Let the great nations contribute much of their arsenals in kind to the world government at agreed valuations in place of cash payment of assessments. Let the world government distribute its arsenal at strategic locations throughout the world, primarily in lands of great powers but at sites under control of the world president, and let the legislature have worldwide inspection powers to make sure that the great powers do not rebuild their own arsenals or other powers build new ones.

Madness, of course, but madness is relative. This madness is nothing compared to the madness of the alternatives, the madness of nuclear war or the madness of unilateral disarmament. Make no mistake; no matter how much you may think today's brinkmanship is necessary, brinkmanship has always eventually ended in war. Moreover, do not sell my madness short. I have complete confidence that if a messenger from outer space convinced the leaders of the world that an invasion of the earth by forces from another planet was imminent, it would not be long before the world leaders would have one commander-in-chief of the arsenals of the world.

As I anticipate some aversion to my concept of having membership in the congress, in effect, bought by the highest-bidding nation, it may be helpful to note this concept is not without precedent and justification. The power of the purse was the means by which the English House of Commons gained its opportunity to share control of the government with the Tudor monarchs. I doubt not that the power of the purse has an effect in our own elections today. Besides, this concept may not be all bad. The Bible tells us where your treasure is, there will your heart be. Psychiatrists never cease to overwhelm me with their ability, almost convincingly, to point out that payment of their high fees is absolutely necessary in order for their therapy to effect a cure. Moreover, as a practical matter, the tendency for a nation to overvalue its assets in order to grab a bigger piece of the representation is balanced by disenfranchisement for as long as possibly eight years on nonpayment of its share of the annual budget during any of such eight years, a share that can substantially increase during such period if other member nations default or if world conditions require emergency assessments or increased annual assessments.

I have left to an ad hoc committee the procedural task of constituting the first congress and to the congress such task for successive congresses. A logician might expect to have difficulty in submitting for his nation an unattested statement of assets from which such fantastic or dire consequences may result, the gamut running from world rule to national bankruptcy. My experience convinces me, however, that throughout the world and throughout history man has never lacked risk takers. It should enliven the cautious political process to see the innovators try to decide whether the seats should be bought by sealed bids, that is, by a statement of assets that cannot be altered even after you see that the statement of assets submitted by a nation with whom you compete entitles it to more seats than does your statement, or by auction, that is, by multiple statements of assets, which are changed until the major nations are in agreement as to the numbers of their respective representations, or by some other method. At some point the founders will have to terminate the process and obtain commitments for whatever annual assessments the nations are willing to pay.

The size of the legislature has carefully been kept manageable for reasons I have previously mentioned, but provision has been made for the potential representation of all the nations through regional groupings, limited to one representative per group in order to prevent any such group's taking over the world government. Admittedly, two large nations could form one new nation in an attempt to avoid this limitation, but in this situation the approval of the congress is required. A distinction has been made not only between member nations and nonmember nations, but also between voting member nations and nonvoting member nations. This gives those nations who cannot afford a seat in the congress and who have been unable to work out an affordable group representation the benefit as member nations of the nonvoting rights given voting nations upon their submitting statements of assets and agreeing their nations and their citizens will accept the burdens of membership other than those of meeting assessments and military quotas.

I would expect funding commitments would be received from at least all of the nations represented in the ad hoc committee, either from single nations or from groups of such nations. I believe such commitments would make this world government viable. I would hope for a larger number of voting nations as well as for a large number of nonvoting members who join even though they cannot afford voting memberships at the time. So the one crucial substantive duty I have left to the ad hoc committee is the decision as to how many nations of the world must ratify this constitution in order that it become established.

I have given the congress the option of electing from its membership two seats at large in the congress for renewable four-year terms. The holders of such seats would be relieved, if they wish to be, from any national allegiance. My hope, perhaps naive, is that this would give the congress the opportunity to retain the services of gifted members and the gifted members the incentive as statesmen to rise above national short-term political expediencies.

New nations may be unable to obtain voting membership in the congress for as long as eight years. This provision evidences an attempt to avoid more frequent reapportionments and gives the congress time to decide whether or not the new nation would be an acceptable voting nation or member of a voting group of neighboring nations.

There is no penalty other than loss of franchise for any nation's not paying assessments or filling its military quota, with one exception. At the time of constituting the first congress and at the times of reconstituting the congress every eighth year, nations who have stated they will pay their assessments must honor the commitment to make the first annual payment. Otherwise the government would never get started. Any dishonoring of such commitment must be penalized, for example, by the congress's providing that the reneging nation must make up such payment before it could ever become a member nation or, if already a member nation, before it could ever again become a member nation. On the other hand, poor nations or nations that for one reason or another do not wish to contribute money or military personnel are encouraged to submit statements of assets and agree to be bound by the world constitution and its laws in order to have the other benefits accruing to member nations. Any such nation not doing so in time before the first meeting of the congress forfeits its automatic right to membership and must be thereafter approved by the congress for membership, as in the case of any new nation.

Although the designation of the member of the congress is left to the nation that holds the seat in the congress, when a vacancy occurs in the congress it is the responsibility of the executive authority of the nation(s) whose seat it is promptly to fill such vacancy so that there is a functioning congress whenever the congress is in session. Any failure to carry out such responsibility subjects the national executive(s) to world court sanctions.

So much for article 1, "The Legislative Department." Article 2, titled "The Executive Department," is next. It is ironic that I who detest being pushed around now find myself creating potentially the most tyrannical office the world has ever seen. I certainly had no idea when I started writing these chapters that my thought process would shove me into this on my quest for a philosophically anarchical society. Hamilton's customarily incisive logic was what drove me to it. He simply said that a weak government is a contradiction in terms, so the enforcer, the executive, shall be single and strong. The Federalist authors' reading of history convinced them that executive tyranny was less to be feared than legislative tyranny, as the former was limited by the scope of the grant of legislative authority and the latter had not yet been checked in history by the concepts of written constitutions, bills of rights, and judicial review, about which more will be said in discussing article 3, titled "The Judicial Department." So I have given the executive enforcement authority within narrow constitutional limits, especially with respect to limitations on the lawmaking authority of the congress, and I have left with the member nations most governmental authority, which I call sovereignty.

You will find few surprises in article 2. The world president has great power. He is the commander in chief of the military forces of the world and of its arsenal. As such he controls all hot lines. Let us contemplate how devasting it would be for a Russian to be elected the first world president. My first observation is that, as Russia does wrong things so well and as we do right things so poorly, and as my earlier chapters conclude that government can do no good, logically a Russian presidency, with its hard negative approach, if within rigid constitutional checks, might be the quickest way to have all people outgrow the need for any government. I have the checks in place. The world congress has inspection, investigative, and rule-making powers. It controls the size of the military, its weaponry, and its activity and pays for this on an annual basis. My second observation is even more devious and intriguing. I can remember at the time of World War II, when I was a recent law school graduate, how some of my independent-thinking, well-educated friends astounded me with bold pronouncements that the United States and its allies would lose the war by winning it. For after the war they would have the burden and hence the cost of ruling the world, so the countries who would prosper in the future would be the losers. Without a trace of judgmental irritation, I ask you to look at the rise of West Germany and Japan. Therefore, as long as the world government has no power to tax—and I have provided that it does not—it follows that the nation that is willing to pay for the cost of the world government by "buying" the seats in the congress that elects the world president comes out ahead, win or lose. If it is successful in winning the election, it has the right to rule the world; if it is unsuccessful, it can, if it chooses, avoid the cost. Less cynically, I would expect those who lose the election would continue in the legislature in order to keep the constitutional limitations in force.

Before leaving the executive provisions, I must point out that although they have been structured so that the world government itself should not be able to become tyrannical, conceivably they could help a tyrannical nation remain in power. This danger presents the same type of problem that our country struggles with daily when in order to have peace and stability in the neighborhood it has been accused of supporting what are called banana republics, small nations that are run by dictators. The trick here is to remember that each nation retains its sovereignty over its peoples. We expect the voting nations will from time to time group together in parties and factions for voting purposes. Such factions may often be held together by common ideologies. They may seek to aid member and nonmember nations whose leadership has similar ideologies. Despite all this, however, the congress should at all times use its broad powers to repel invasions, contain insurrections, prevent foreign interference in domestic affairs, prohibit unauthorized national armies and alliances, and control arms shipments. Thus only will it be possible for each nation to work out its own destiny.

The writing of article 3, titled "The Judicial Department," gave me more trouble than anything else yet in the writing of this book. The reason is that with the judiciary the concept of checks and balances comes a cropper. The executive, with his power to initiate and enforce international policy, act as commander in chief, make judicial appointments, and veto legislation, and the legislative branch, with its power to tell the executive most of what he can do, give him the money to do it, and impeach him if he strays too far, both have the power to hold in check abuse by the other, but when the ultimate checker, the supreme court, declares null and void an action of the executive or an act of the congress, who checks the checker? No one, for as Jefferson, who saw this opening for unbridled power, noted, impeachment in this situation is scarcely a scarecrow, and, I might add, nor is the tedious and time-consuming amendment process a remedy. Think of it. In our government, which boasts that it is a government of, by, and for *all* the people, one very learned man on a Supreme Court that is split five to four, *one* person paradoxically may be able to command a quarter of a billion others to obey his will in a matter such as abortion. Even the much maligned pope has no such power, even when infallibly he speaks the Word of God.

Under these circumstances please humor my thinking of all this in a personal way. Is this one learned old man (I keep calling him learned hoping you will follow my example and call me learned also rather than senile) going to be able to tell the world with binding authority the meaning of the provisions of my world constitution, which I have drafted with such great pains, going to be able, so to speak, to tell me what I have said or, even worse, what I meant to say? After all, there certainly is nothing impeachable about a learned old man telling people what I was trying to say, especially if he waits until after my death to do so. My ego revolts. If I provide that the world constitution and the laws of the world congress are the supreme law of the world and the supreme court shall declare such law, then though I am one who does not like to be pushed around, I have created the ultimate pusher, an institution that could harbor a Frankenstein, one learned old monster with the unbridled power to tell the whole world what to do. Even after calm reflection I believe it has been in this area of judicial review that the U.S. Constitution has undergone its greatest strain in my lifetime and I believe most of the founding fathers did not contemplate the magnitude of this problem or the illogic in having the unchecked few thus rule the many in a democracy. Why didn't they? My answer is because the law was fundamentally different in 1787 and, equally important, the law was perceived differently than it is today.

Let us first look at the state of the law in 1787. Since earliest times, people have always had a strong sense of individual justice. As busy executive and legislative bodies have not had the time to be bothered with it, some other way had to be found to dispense it. As an aside, personally I think this individual sense of justice may be inborn. I remember a Sunday family dinner I attended years ago. Present at the table were parents of middle years, their little daughter who was almost able to talk, and several college students whom the father coached. Dessert was ice cream and when the little one compared the size of her portion to that of the others she began to cry. Nothing could stop her until I first, followed by the others, equalized her portion with spoonfuls from our plates. Minutes later, when our plates were mostly empty and hers remained relatively untouched, she began to cry again. Nothing could stop her until we again equalized the portions by taking back spoonfuls for our plates.

In the history of England the first trials were by water, by fire, by battle, or by some other ordeal in which the accused or his stand-in benefactor was subjected to some test. If the one thus tried survived the accused was declared to be not guilty. Upon the coming of trial by a jury of one's equals the English judges appointed by the king started making the common law of England by deciding each local dispute in the same manner that some judge had decided a comparable prior case and then by writing all this down so that future judges could apply the same law to a future case involving similar facts. Moreover, the ultimate source of the law declared in each case, express or implied, was metaphysically found to be in the laws of nature or of nature's God. As medievalist Bracton wrote: "We are not under man but under God and the law." This was the status of the law and the way society looked at it in 1787.

The 1787 U.S. Constitution, however, contained an entirely new legal concept. It related to the manner in which the losing party might be able to appeal an adverse decision in the lower courts. In England the court of final appeal was the House of Lords, the senior branch of the English Parliament, whose members and the eldest sons of deceased members, all landed nobility, were appointed by the king or, more likely, by a prior king. The founding fathers had just fought a war to rid themselves of monarchy and nobility. They had to find another final court of appeal. They did so by creating the Supreme Court and in so doing paid the concept little attention. In fairness, the enabling philosophers such as Locke and Montesquieu were also not much concerned with the judiciary. This is understandable in the case of those philosophers, because a judiciary that ultimately answers to a branch of the legislature and reaches its decisions logically by the case method pegged to natural law was what they had lived with and has an obvious stability. In creating the judicial branch, however, headed by its own final court of appeal and at the same time in keeping with the common law of England based on natural law, the founding fathers without premeditation gave this branch both a separate autonomy and a metaphysical support that are not to be found in either of the other two branches. This consideration has given and continues to give our country serious problems, as we are now going at great length to see.

Any physicist can demonstrate how nature abhors a vacuum and how into a vacuum once it is created practically anything may rush. As metaphysicist I shall now demonstrate how human nature abhors a vacuum in belief and how into such a vacuum once it has been created hot air and much more have rushed. We live today in a secular society, a society that takes pride in having outgrown myths, metaphysics, idols, and icons, yet I see today a greater idol than the world has ever had before, the myth known as "the law." Before I can proceed with an article on the judicial branch I must cast out this myth, this devil, in the same spirit in which a doctor heals the sick. My task is really very easy. The first step is to note that the executive branch—let us call its members tyrants, which originally was a Greek word meaning "lords"—had been defanged of any metaphysical support in the perception of the people of our country by the time of our revolution. In seventeenth-century England the Stuart kings fought and lost the battle to get support for their insistence on the prior historical view that they ruled by divine right. Such defangings take time. In Japan it was not until 1945 that, by victors' mandate, the Japanese emperor, in order to keep his throne, agreed that he was no longer God. Hamilton's requirement for a strong executive was fought and won on the proper premise of necessity.

The second step is to note that the legislative branch in our country, from the nature of the activities of the legislators, has never needed defanging, detonguing perhaps, but not defanging. The word *parliament* comes from the same word as does *parlor* where people *parler,* the French word for "speak." The legislators, having once opened their mouths, bear a closer resemblance to monkeys than to gods.

The third step is to note that the judicial branch never had independent power before 1787 and only slowly dared to use it thereafter, so the defanging process has not yet really begun. People do not yet realize that today they view and accept the law as an idol. Let us test this statement on you. What do you mean when you say "the law"? What is the basis for your comfort in "the law"?

At the start of my legal practice I remember being put down by a layman who questioned my abhorrence of brilliant Justice Douglas. "Why?" he asked.

"Because he doesn't follow precedent," I replied.

"What does he follow?" he asked.

I hesitated and replied, "What he believes to be right."

"What's wrong with that?" he asked and I remained mute.

Now, forty years later, I know what is wrong with that. Today the law is without a standard. Bismarck put it best in saying, "Don't ever let the people see how laws and sausage are made."

The common law had the natural law as its ultimate standard of what was right, and natural law was derived from God. Today there is little left of the logical judge-made common law. Our society believes government can do good. The solution for every problem is a new law or package of laws, called statutes, legislator-made laws. Lobbyists for every interest group seek preferential legislation at every level of rule making, federal, state, and local, both in the legislatures and in the councils, committees, and administrative agencies in all three branches, so that any separation of functions has become obscured. A judge has little chance to decide most cases on the facts. He has to decide most cases on the rules. Prior cases with comparable facts are of little help, as the rules change so frequently. The logical basis of the common law has disappeared. Rule-making bodies are not known for the logic of their promulgations. When the judge merely applies these haphazard and often conflicting rules, one has no right to take any comfort in "the law." Can one even take any comfort from the power of the judge to hold that any such rule is unconstitutional? At first blush one might think the comfort in "the law" is to be found in the provisions of the U.S. Constitution as amended, but it does not work this way. Some judges believe the constitution is a living document that should change with the times, and they interpret it to do just that. Today the law is no more and no less than what the Supreme Court decides that it is, and in a prior chapter we have seen how one can rationalize anything.

Another reason for not taking comfort in the law is its ever-increasing complexity. Not only are new rules enacted daily, but also the enacting bodies must document their every action in the enactment process in order to be able to evidence in court, if the enactment is questioned, that it was enacted in accordance with due process of law. So we have created a monster that feeds on itself and unless soon altered may fall of its own weight, *mole ruit sua*. Today the law in action is an expense of time in a waste of shame. Unfortunately, people still see it as something more than the will of the Supreme Court. The law has not yet been defanged. It has idolized itself and its Talmudic subtle nuances. In answer to a justice whose opinion merely reflected what the justice thought to be right, Justice Frankfurter's opinion stated that this court does not sit like a Mohammedan cadi under some tree in Arabia dispensing justice according to the exigencies of the moment. What Frankfurter failed to add was that the court sits like solipsists on an elevated bench, seriously, haughtily, and graciously dispensing justice after much writing and more research according to what each judge believes the law should be. This translates into the same thing as the cadi's exigency of the moment, except on a much higher and often obfuscating level and after a longer period of time.

But this sameness has not been generally perceived. Why? What happened was the creation of an enormous vacuum of belief into which rushed the myth of the law. With the defanging of the executive and legislative branches all that was left for the people to believe in was the judiciary. But the law lost its standard when it ceased to look to God as its source. This process culminated with the coming of the doctrine of the separation of church and state. The court developed this doctrine over the years from interpretations of the establishment clause in the constitution, interpretations that I believe are correct and, in a pluralistic society, necessary. Although the law's standard perished, the defanging of the law never took place, as the people refused to give up their dream of good government and social justice. So their desire to do good through their government has caused the hot air and other attributes of the legal process in the name of "the law" to rush in to fill the vacuum in belief. Today our society's perception of the law is in transition. On the one hand, people have great expectations of "the law" because they idolize it as the undefanged metaphysical source of social justice. On the other hand, increasingly they are witnessing the abuses caused by "the law" through their newly found perception of the absolute authority and independence of the Supreme Court. The solution, of course, is philosophical anarchy, but as its joyful day has not yet arrived, I have had to write in my world constitution an unidealized judiciary article that I hope you will approach critically, pragmatically, and profanely, without fear of fangs, as I am not pleased with it.

Here are the options that I considered for my world government: (1) no judiciary, (2) a minor judiciary with the ultimate appeal to the congress; and (3) a judiciary that is an equal third branch of the government with its own supreme court, following the example of the U.S. Constitution.

Option #1. No judiciary. I started with the three branch concept for reasons previously mentioned. The congress is to make the laws and the executive to enforce them. But why do I need a judiciary to interpret them? After all, my government is composed of nations, not people, and its purpose is limited to the maintenance of peace between nations. Let all the problems of individual rights and justice continue to be handled by the individual nations with respect to their own peoples. I do not need another layer of government on top of the excessive layers we now have. If the executive gets out of hand, the congress has adequate controls; if the congress gets out of hand, the executive has adequate power. I do not need a judiciary.

Reluctantly I discarded this concept, for two reasons:

1. Hamilton convinced me that a mere confederation of nations will not prevent war. With a confederation, if a nation breaks the international law, the only way to punish it is to start a war against it. To avoid this outcome it is necessary to have people subject to the sanctions of magistrate courts and, in particular, those leaders who break the international law, whether on behalf of their nations or on a frolic of their own. This requirement makes a judicial department necessary.
2. The history behind the first ten amendments to the U.S. Constitution, known as the Bill of Rights, convinced me that the so-called freedom-loving nations of the world would not accept my constitution without provisions assuring the people of the world that the world government would not deprive them of certain rights.

You will remember the Hamiltonian federalists saw no need for a bill of rights because the constitution left all authority in the sovereign states except that given to the federal government, whereas the Jeffersonian republicans refused to accept the constitution until they were assured that the bill of rights would be added. This requirement of a bill of rights makes a judicial department necessary.

Option #2. Minor judiciary with the ultimate appeal to the congress. I have always liked the common-law system of Elizabethan England. As previously mentioned, the king and Parliament, executive and legislature, ruled, and the senior house in the legislature, the House of Lords, the hereditary nobility, decided the key legal issues that arose on appeal from the common-law courts. After all, if the congress can make the laws, why shouldn't they be their ultimate interpreters? The answer lies in the difference between the English and U.S. systems. A written constitution having rights flowing to the people that is interpreted by a supreme legislature is no constitution at all and, hence, no security against encroachment by the government through the legislature on the liberties of the people. But, I argued with myself, the congress can avoid the constitution by initiating the amendment process. Then I remembered I had provided that any amendment would have to be ratified by three-quarters of the member nations, a cumbersome process not to be recommended. No, the congress could not be the court of final appeal.

Option #3. Judiciary that is an equal third branch of the government. You will find few surprises in article 3, "The Judiciary Department," as necessity has compelled me to use the U.S. Constitution as my model, for want of something better. Yet I shall continue to find it ironic that our democracy, which purports to be the rule of all of the people, has centered such potential for absolute power in so few. There is one observation, however, I think can be made in rational support of a supreme judiciary. By education and environment judges have a different perspective from legislators and executives that may bring a certain stability to a government. I shall dramatize this difference with two stories.

In today's corporate world it never ceases to irritate me how regularly CEOs engage in the customary business practice of having their appointees, the general counsels to the corporation, make many unpopular business decisions purportedly as a matter of law in situations where no prohibiting legal issue is involved. Have you not heard the expression: "I'd like to do that, but my lawyers say I can't"? I consider such legal activity to be barratrous, an abuse of the legal process. Law, like insurance and armies, best serves its purpose when present but unused. The civilized approach is not intentionally to set a fire to get the worth of your premium or to start a war to get the worth of the cost of your army, and it should not be to get the worth of the cost of your lawyers by having them make the unpopular business decisions. The law is in enough disrepute without its having to bear the burden of being responsible for unpopular business decisions. Yet, pragmatically, I confess I feel this practice often may be in the best interest of the corporation, because CEOs have such superegos, such a personal need to be accepted as leaders, that alone they might not be able to say no. Likewise, it may well be in the best interest of any government if it has a judiciary appointed for life. Judges can say no far more easily than can executives and legislators, who must deal with lobbyists whose organizations have contributed so much toward enabling these officials to obtain their short-term positions and whose organizations' continuing contributions are so necessary for the reelections of these officials.

The second story is nothing more than a visual aid. Picture, if you will please, a balance scale suspended from a beam by means of an elastic cord. Justice and fairness require only that the scales be in equipose. These virtues are not concerned with how low the scales sink so long as they remain in equipose. Said differently, it is unjust for one lady to have 3,000 pairs of shoes, but a confiscatory fixed-rate state income tax hitting all uniformly is not unjust in this sense, and so the happening of the former unsettles a populace and a society more than the latter. Thus a constitution, as it applies to everyone, is less likely to be enforced selectively by judges than it is by legislators who can pass private selective laws or by the executive who can easily enforce laws selectively. ("Everybody else was going sixty miles per hour, but I alone got a ticket.") So the judicial branch is the least likely to act unfairly and hence unsettlingly.

Finally, the judicial process usually does not move as fast as the processes of the other branches. It also is a more orderly process, with its time-honored procedural traditions. By reason of lifetime appointments judges usually are older than the average legislators and executives. Reflection, orderliness, and age tend to have a stabilizing influence.

Incidentally, legalists may be surprised I have required the losing party to pay in advance the full court costs of any civil litigation. They may even accuse me of dispensing "bought" justice. My reply is that the squeaking wheel always gets the most grease, so there is no reason why the one who squeaks unnecessarily should not pay.

The remaining articles of the constitution are primarily procedural and speak for themselves except for article 7, titled "The Bill of Rights." Previously I have discussed why I have included a bill of rights. In order to be able to subject people to the jurisdictions of the world courts for criminal violation of the world constitution and of the enabling laws of the world congress, it is necessary that these individuals have individual protections such as due process of law. Another reason for including a bill of rights is that I envision more people becoming subject to the jurisdiction of the world courts in future years as the nations increase the scope of the activities of the world government through the constitutional amendment process. For example, besides already mentioned amendments with respect to naturalization and immigration I would expect much can be said for involving the world government in such matters as international commerce, monetary systems, postal systems, copyrights, counterfeiting, and bankruptcies.

With respect to the Bill of Rights itself I have proceeded on a two-pronged approach, that of protecting man's right to be left alone and that of protecting his right to speak out. With respect to the specific rights, I shall comment only on those that I believe are very controversial. The most controversial right, involving the right to be left alone, is that involving freedom from conscription. The world congress may not require military service. I shall first discuss this concept practically and then theoretically. Practically, it is without meaning. As we have seen, fulfillment of the military quotas for the armed forces of the world is a requirement placed upon the sovereign voting nations who, to obtain and keep their voting power, must fill their apportioned quotas by voluntary enlistment, mandatory draft, or otherwise as each nation sees fit. Once nationally selected personnel, volunteer or conscript, take the oath of allegiance to the world government, they subject themselves to the world military courts. Theoretically, however, the significance of this freedom from conscription is great. History reveals that the two principal supports for any tyrant are his power to tax the people and his power to conscript his armies. I just want a prohibition of both such powers in place in my constitution in order that my new world government will not easily be led into future temptation. I wonder whether you will like my rationale for this bold and innovative stroke. Please read on and see.

For a moment let us talk about equality. I believe God loves you as much as he loves me, that is, he loves us equally as I try to love my children equally. I believe the law should treat each person equally, what is called the equal protection of the laws, and I have never believed separate is equal. I also believe we are all different and God gave us different talents that he wants us to use in different walks of life. John Adams, overstating, made this point in a curt exchange of letters he had with his wife, Abigail, in Quincy, Massachusetts, when he was working on the drafting of the constitution in Philadelphia. In a letter to him she had complained that the news coming out of Philadelphia made no mention of women having the right to vote. She told him to put it in the constitution or she would lead a women's revolt that would make the men's past little Tea Party look like a tempest in a teapot. To this he replied: "Your letter contained not one word about the children. Children who are allowed to grovel are closer to animals than to children of God." When I look at our country's popular spectator sports today and see the violence of legal tackles, blocks, and ball-strippings and the number of serious injuries, I can conclude only that some like to fight more than I do, so let us let them do so and let us pay what it takes to get volunteers. Remember, not many will be needed, because the purpose of the world government is to avoid nuclear wars and a space race and to abolish national armies, substituting instead a world military force of only the size necessary to maintain the peace of the world.

I have just reread the above paragraph a little over a year after it was written. Although I stand by every word of it, it does strike a chord that leaves sounding a mercenary overtone that I must cut off. This book is about voluntary and mandatory communities and points up their differences and the importance of understanding these differences if we want a better world. It is not a book about those we esteem in both communities, the saints and the heroes, respectively. I do not forget the importance of the saints in witnessing against evil for righteousness' sake or the importance of the heroes in witnessing against injustice for necessity's sake. As somebody said: "Exhilarating is the holiness of the saint and the courage of the hero; grievous is the sacrifice of the saint and the privation of the hero."

Now returning to the Bill of Rights, freedom of speech is a much more difficult right to grant than the freedom to be left alone, because any speaker requires a listener, just as any thud from a falling tree requires an ear. What if the ear wants to hear not? What if it wants to be left alone? Years ago I read a judicial opinion in which members of a religious group were convicted under an anti-litter ordinance for passing out tracts in a public place, and I was disappointed in the court because it did not even point out that the actual offenders, the litterers, were those who accepted the tracts only to drop them on the sidewalk rather than to reject them in the first place. Freedom of speech poses tough issues. I suspect it would take years to find any integrated explanation of its meaning in the volumes of lengthy opinions of the U.S. Supreme Court that have been handed down on the issue. Fortunately, the only way the issue becomes relevant in my world constitution is in respect to sedition. I have carefully defined treason to require proof of overt physical acts—a smoking gun or a dog's first bite—so I would hope the world congress and judiciary would make no attempt to punish or restrict free speech, except in extreme cases, such as security leaks by personnel of the world government, and, in general, would leave this problem with the sovereign nations. Consequently, I have included in the Bill of Rights freedom of speech and freedom of publication. No matter how clear and present the danger, let the people talk and write all they want and let the policing of this talking and writing continue to be a national problem. Sticks and stones will break my bones, but names will never hurt me.

I have substituted freedom of publication for freedom of press. Freedom of the press implies a right to have access to the news, whereas freedom of publication merely adds to the freedom to talk the freedom to write. Here follows my rationale for this substitution. Jefferson said the two worst things in our country—both necessary—were its government and its press, but that if he could have only one he would choose the press. I appreciate his thought, but I come out the other way in connection with my very limited world government. I have hardly ever read a news article in the press on a subject about which I had firsthand knowledge without being either horrified or saddened by the difference between what the article said the situation was and what I knew it to be. In a search for the security of the world I am personally choosing government over the press. In an attempt to keep expenses down, I do not want to impose on the world congress the cost of giving the people of the world a media circus, lest we achieve, before my sixth form of government, one to be added to Plato's five called mediocrity but spelled *mediacracy*. My constitution contemplates a confederation of nations. The world congress has been given the power to obtain from the world executive all necessary information. The world congress and the member nations can decide what freedom to give the press and the media.

I also have omitted the rights of freedom of assembly and of petition. The function of the world government is to abolish warfare between nations. The world government is not to be a supergovernment. It is not to redress the grievances of the people. Let those who still believe they can do good through mandatory government and who must protest do so at the national level. For the same reason I have included not only the customary prohibition against the establishment of religion, but also prohibitions against the establishment of an economic system, education, health, and welfare. Finally, consistent with the retention of sovereignty in the nations, the requirement that certain decent judicial procedures be followed and in all cases with due process of law applies only to the world government and does not purport to apply to the member nations. In other words, I have included the equivalent of the Fifth but not the Fourteenth Amendment. I hope you will look at and like my world constitution.

Here end my comments on a world government that we need. Next to come, after a year-end break, will be my comments on our country's government, of which we need less.

Chapter IX
On the Book of Job

I found the last chapter to be both challenging and exhausting. So it is fitting for both writer and reader to have a rest. Before tackling the next major project for this book, namely, the setting forth of unnecessary activities of our government today, I am here inserting a letter I wrote my sons in college in 1983 as a variation on the themes of this book:

Dear Andy and David,

David, the reason for this letter is to thank Andy for telling me last Sunday to read George Orwell's essay, "Politics and the English Language." He said I'd love it. Last Monday mother bought a collection of his essays. Tuesday morning I read the fifteen-page essay. I loved it. The son knows the father. The reason for sending this letter to you also is to share with you the thoughts that this essay inspired.

Andy, congratulations! You are now well on your way to belonging in the select company of educated men, a company which in every generation is very small, a company which in the generations of my life has been smaller than in certain past ages and which today is smaller than in my childhood.

First, I must tell David the point Orwell makes. He says today's sloppy thinking produces sloppy writing and sloppy writing can produce sloppy thinking in others so that present political chaos is connected with the decay of language, and polysyllabic Latin abstractions and pretentious sentence structures make lies sound truthful and murder respectable.

Orwell says a scrupulous writer, in every sentence he writes, will ask himself four questions, thus:

What am I trying to say?
What words will express it?
What image or idiom will make it clearer?
Is the image fresh enough to be effective?

He will never use a metaphor or other figure of speech that he is used to seeing in print or a long word where a short one will do. He will prefer the concrete, the simple, and the precise to the abstract and convoluted, the active voice to the passive, and, for example, the common names for plants and animals to the scientific names for flora and fauna.

Orwell uses most of the fifteen pages to analyze intellectual-sounding paragraphs of political propaganda and to reveal their naked nonsense. To be able to recognize such stuff is one mark of an educated man. Hence my congratulations, Andy.

The part of the essay I liked most was the discussion of worn-out metaphors, which you should never use, especially those so worn-out that the original image is lost, such as "tow the line" for "toe the line." My favorite, as you know, is "by the skin of one's teeth," a very narrow margin ("escaped by the skin of my teeth"—Job 19:20 [R.S.V.]). Let us look at this metaphor. How much skin is on your teeth? To escape by nothing must mean not to escape. This is nonsense. Has the original image been lost?

I rushed to my favorite reference work, *Fowler's Modern English Usage* (Oxford University Press), which upon request I will gladly send either or both of you. Under "skin" appears: "With the skin of my teeth; see 'Misquotation.' " Under "Misquotation" appears:

> The correct words of a few familiar sayings that are more often wrongly than rightly quoted may be useful. The misquoting of phrases that have survived on their own merits out of little read authors . . . is a very venial offense; and indeed it is almost a pedantry to use the true form instead of so established a wrong one; it would be absurd to demand that no-one should ever use a trite quotation without testing its verbal accuracy. . . . But when a quotation comes from such a source as a well-known play of Shakespeare, or "Lycidas," or the Bible, or Prayer Book, to give it wrongly at least requires excuse, and any great prevalence of such misquotation would prove us discreditably ignorant of our own literature.

Fowler concludes this passage by pointing out that such words as "I am escaped by the skin of my teeth" are often so much more used than the true form, "I am escaped with the skin of my teeth," that their accuracy is sure to be taken for granted unless occasional attempts like the present are made to draw attention to them.

Inspired by Orwell, I shall now show how this continued incorrect use of a worn-out metaphor has produced sloppy religious thinking in others so that they have suffered bad leaders willingly and thereby weakened the Christian witness in my lifetime in my country.

To be able to do this we must have a common starting point. When Andy first attended church about the age of four, Mr. Hughes, sitting behind us, commented favorably on how wonderfully unusual it was to see such a young child in church. I replied I wanted Andy to learn how to believe before he learned how to think. Now that you are at college you should think and you should doubt. Hence, our common starting point will be a here-unanswered question:

Will you be able through your entire life to ignore the hungry, the homeless and clothesless, the sick, the prisoner, and the ignorant?

Before you answer this question, you should consider what would be nice (the ideal) and what is necessary (the real), and you should consider what those who are not able to ignore these unfortunates are doing about it, because this also will affect you.

In order to help you answer, I shall divide all people into groups. I shall write with bold black and white strokes for clarity of perception, and hopefully at times with a touch of the grosbeak's rose for beauty, because such groupings in life are seen as various shades of the female's gray-browns, making identification difficult.

Most people do not think about the unfortunates, either because of inability to think or because of lack of time, which they spend in work or in pleasure or in both. The few who think about the problem of the unfortunates are two types: those who believe something can be done about them and those who believe nothing can be. Of those who believe something can be done to help the unfortunates, with few exceptions, they have all used the force of armies or the force of laws to carry out their will, with the support or the apathy of the nonthinking multitudes. How badly they have succeeded today and throughout history you will learn yourself if you join the select company of educated men.

Since this last sentence is controversial, I shall mention a few insights in passing. First, I suppose many would agree that the scientists have taken the joy out of war, whose heroes are no longer admired like Robin Hood. Second, I suppose few would agree that the law does not help the unfortunates because today—and I use abstractions that Orwell would deplore in order to make the lie sound truthful—law and justice are synonymous. Yet it is no coincidence that the lawyers whose god, if you were to describe him with a secular abstraction, would be called the law are, regrettably, often hated people. I say "regrettably" because in order to have a better world we should not kill all the lawyers; we should kill the idea that law can solve any problem. At best the law merely defers or transfers the outward manifestations of problems; it is today's foremost necessary evil.

The only thinker and leader I know who helped the unfortunates without using force is Jesus. He told his followers to feed the hungry, to heal the sick, and to cast out devils (his way, I believe, of saying: to educate the ignorant). The Christian message has three key points:

1. We are God's agents. As the shortest sermon says in just ten two-lettered words: if it is to be it is up to me.
2. We are to do the will of God. We are not to follow our own will or the will of other men, because man's will, man's way, man's armies, and man's laws have never helped the unfortunates. We learn God's will for us by talking with God (prayer) and by listening to Scripture and to the teachings of the church. Then we follow Jesus and try to do what he would do.
3. If we keep our faith that this is the way to bring God's kingdom to earth here and now and to witness to our faith through our work, then no matter what happens we will receive God's peace and God's grace because God loves us. Grace means concurrent forgiveness for our sins.

I have presented the key points positively and affirmatively but, in deciding how you can answer our question—can you ignore those who suffer?—remember also that Christianity helps us save time, effort, and expense in avoiding improper ways of helping the unfortunates. During the Great Depression of the 1930s, the beggars would come to the rectory door. My mother would race my father to reach it because he would give the requested quarter for a bite to eat, a quarter we could not afford, but she would ask the beggar to go to the back door, where she would make him a sandwich. This continued until once, when my father beat my mother to the front door, she stealthily followed the beggar with our quarter to the illegal saloon in the next block. Jesus never said give money to the poor.

Now let us return to the wondrous story of Job. Job was an exceedingly healthy, wealthy, and wise man with a wonderful family. He lost his health, wealth, and most of his family, really everything but his life itself. His friends could not understand why he continued to have faith in God. They thought he must have sinned against God and was being punished. At the end of the story Job regained his health, wealth, and the happy remaining members of his family. The biblical experts say no one knows the meaning of the Book of Job.

Let me add to the story of Job two thoughts: first, the thought so beautifully expressed in that awesome verse from the Book of Ecclesiastes, thus: "I returned and saw under the sun, that the race is not to the swift, nor the battle to the strong, neither yet bread to the wise, nor riches to men of understanding, nor yet favor to men of skill; but time and chance happeneth to them all."

Secondly, in the introduction to the Book of Job in the Jerusalem Bible we are told the concept of a future life was a later development and it was St. Paul who emphasized the good would be rewarded in heaven.

Now I submit that the guts of Christianity is following the will of God and the way of Jesus in helping the unfortunates here and now, and having faith in the process. Spending time trying to understand the accidents of life·

(miscalled Acts of God) other than from a scholar's scientific perspective or thinking about rewards and punishments in this world or the next is really not helping the unfortunates.

Let us at long last return to our worn-out metaphor. I ask what use of language helps the reader better understand the guts of Christianity:

1. The correct metaphor: When the devil had taken from Job his wealth, health, and family, Job escaped with only the skin of his teeth (i.e., with absolutely nothing) and kept his faith. Job knew time and chance have nothing to do with man's following the will of God.

   or

2. The incorrect metaphor: As Job had escaped by the skin of his teeth, God had rewarded him—the margin was narrow after all he had been through—and so maybe God will reward us, if not here, then in heaven.

My conclusion is that sloppy writing (the nonsense in #2) produces sloppy thinking and that thinking Christians should not let their churches and their leaders be so misled, as this otherworldly emphasis takes the church away from where its action should be: "Seek ye first the kingdom of God and his righteousness" (God's way of governing here and now to take care of his unfortunates).

I love you,
Daddy

Chapter X
On Christianity and Democracy

This is the beginning of my second year of retirement. Gone is the fear lest I not transcribe in a timely manner the insights that a working lifetime had suppressed. The outline is in order. Man needs physical, mental, and spiritual food. The hope is for each man to fill his own needs. When he cannot, then first family, next voluntary community, and finally mandatory community take over. In taking over, these communities operate on as local and autonomous a level as is possible without endangering their unifying effectiveness. The goal is for each man to be able to fill his own needs without preventing any other man from reaching the goal. The means for attaining the goal is to solve every problem in life at the simplest and, if possible, at a voluntary level. Throughout one's lifetime, this activity should be supported by a belief that eventually the goal is attainable.

With the need for haste gone, I took some time off from writing to do some reading. I reread the Bible in several different translations, as well as some current commentaries. This left me with an impression that differs from that I had held since my youth. This new impression posed a problem. Should I revise the chapters written last year? I decided not to. No fundamental change in outlook had taken place. But these comments are appropriate at this time.

The one fact about Jesus that I was never told in church was that he was willing to accept criticism of himself. It was only with respect to the holy spirit that criticism was forbidden. He (the holy spirit) is invincible and inviolable—unstoppable, as this autobiographical story witnesses.

Upon my return to Philadelphia after an internment of four years in wilderness camps during World War II, I looked up my college tutor in the old Bellevue Stratford hotel, where he was attending a convention. Over a brandy in the bar he fired up his prewar tutee with this delightful story. The week before, a returning ensign who was seeking admission to the college of which my tutor had become president entered his office with a problem. Since childhood the ensign had always dreamt of becoming a doctor. But the war left him with the loss of an eye. His advisers were now all advising him to enter a profession with fewer reading demands. At that point in the story my tutor looked at me and said, "I then did this." Whereupon he took out his glass eye, flipped it toward the ceiling, caught it, replaced it, and said, "It never stopped me."

Mindful that Jesus could tolerate criticism of himself, here are things about Jesus that the Gospels emphasized, my childhood training did not, and I dislike:

1. I dislike his speaking in parables. Jesus spoke on occasion directly only to the twelve apostles and implied he would continue thus to speak only to Peter's successors, the hierarchy. Incidentally, I hope you wondered whether I caught the double entendre when the Harvard professor described Christianity as parabolic. I did not. I wonder whether Crane Brinton did. In any event, I like to be spoken to directly. A good image or idiom

for clarification is permissible, even desirable, but a parable to hide the meaning reminds me of Plato's dislike of rhetoric, which can stand in the way of logic as salesmanship and advertising can stand in the way of education. Could it be that the times required Jesus to conceal his meaning for fear of premature persecution? If so, our democracy is to be commended for allowing me to voice belief in philosophical anarchy without fear of certification, the English word for a lunacy commission.

2. I dislike his emphasis upon miracles over teachings. The Sermon on the Mount in recognizable detail appears only in two of the Gospels. I suppose my problem is that my own church in my lifetime has changed dramatically. It used to be the body of Christ based upon Scripture, to which had been added the imprint of English tradition, reason, and experience, particularly as reflected in the Book of Common Prayer of 1928. It was a lively and transforming faith in contrast to today's self-centered, long-suffering pietism.

    Remember, I am complaining about emphasis, not about miracles. I believe in miracles. I like another's thought that any coincidence is a minor miracle in which God chooses to remain anonymous. I have always been and still am awed by how my prayers, God willing, have been answered and how, especially when the going gets tough, things happen providentially. But I am a believer because the teachings and example of Jesus provide us with the answer to the problems of man and not because of miracles, which follow belief, and I deplore the church's involving her membership in producing miracles. Man's job is to seek the kingdom and humbly leave the miracles to God.

3. I dislike Jesus' conclusion that the kingdom of God is everlasting life. Jesus starts off all right by proclaiming with John the Baptist that the kingdom of God is at hand, but by the time you reach the Gospel according to St. John you find Jesus substituting for the kingdom of God the concept of everlasting life. I have always found thinking and talking about the afterlife to be irritating, presumptuous, and a waste of time. But as I have pinned so much of my dream for a better world upon my belief in its consistency with the will of God, I realized I had to check out this apparent ambiguity in the nature of the kingdom.

Whenever, in my practice of law, I had to understand a tough legal concept in a hurry I always tried to find an opinion written by Felix Frankfurter on the legal issue involved, because he laid the law out so succinctly and thoroughly. So I picked up some of the works of three excellent, respected, modern-day Protestant theologians, Machem, Barth, and Bultmann, in the hope they would lay out the afterlife just as succinctly and thoroughly as Frankfurter laid out the law. They do. What didactic assurance! Were not I a believer in both Jesus (as God) and the law (as necessary), my attitude toward these writers and Frankfurter would be: what arrogance! The view of the kingdom held by these three experts resembles in no way my view of the kingdom, my dream. Indeed, one of them, as though speaking directly to me, states that the nineteenth-century idea of using Christianity to make a better world is scripturally unsound; the kingdom of God comes only at the end of the world, after a final judgment, for which he uses the insider's word, *eschatology*, the doctrine of last things. Fortunately, he does not pin this revelation on Jesus, whose view of the kingdom, he says, was not detailed; rather, he pins it on prophets and saints in both testaments. So again I find Jesus to be a breath of fresh air coming between the deadly exclusiveness of the Old Testament and of the apostolic writings of the New Testament. Jesus, who when he wanted to could be very precise as to what one should think and do, tells me my first obligation is to seek the kingdom. As he does not fill in the details, he expects me to, in active obedience to all that he stands for. In so doing I shall not be intimidated by details supplied by others using the processes of thinking on matters not subject to the power of thought. (This last phrase is a variation of a great line in, I believe, a book by Rebecca West.) How can you expect books written between 40 and 100 years after the death of Jesus to talk about his kingdom on earth? If only Sam Erwin had been around with his simultaneous prick of the pen to keep the record straight! You will remember the senator, in chairing the Watergate hearings, used these words to express his disgust at the conflicting oral testimony and at the forgetfulness of witnesses who had not seen fit to keep records.

For no matter how you slice it, these modern-day writings are all scriptural interpretations. Interpretations are just that, interpretations, whether of Scripture or of the U.S. Constitution. Damned if I want to follow someone like Ed Meese, who says the constitution can mean no more than what the founding fathers meant it to mean, or someone who says the word of God can mean no more than what the first apostles say is meant, an apostle, for instance, like James, the brother of Jesus, whom Jesus never—well, hardly ever—mentions. Yet I do not want either the constitution or the scriptures to be so livelily living as to resemble an old stump sprouting weeds. Barth helped me here with three insights:

a. I cannot worship God. To do so risks worshiping any illusive abstraction. I can only worship the Word of God, that is, Jesus as revealed by Scripture.
b. God is no mere inner immanence but an outside being.
c. Protestant theology starts at the top and works down, whereas Rome starts at the bottom (where most of the congregation remain) and works up through the hierarchy.

I believe this last insight is another reason for putting the guidance of our voluntary community in the hands of Rome. Someone has to try to understand these holy mysteries to the extent it is given man to understand them, in order to keep the faith pure, but I should not dabble with them.

4. I dislike Jesus' doctrine of the election. "Many are called, but few are chosen," he said. This is the concept I find most objectionable. My philosophical anarchy will not work without the involvement of everybody. So I like Jesus' insistence that the Word of God must first be preached to everybody throughout the world. But why he, the ultimate absolutist, then goes on to say that of all mankind, all sinful, only some, presumably those with relatively few sins but with absolute faith, will enjoy everlasting life rather than eternal damnation I do not know. This smacks of relativism to me. If you argue humanistically that Jesus had to take

this position because everybody could not have everlasting life, I would point out that this is God's problem, not yours or mine. Indeed, I have as much trouble with this doctrine of the election as I do with the concept that in a democracy all should show their lack of discrimination by attending the same public schools except for the intellectually gifted, who, as determined by mere man, may attend special public schools for the gifted. This is the height of discrimination against those whose gifts fall just short of enabling their being among the select.

Perhaps a cathartic diversion will help relieve my trouble. The church boasts that she is Christ's bride. Could this be why I find Jesus henpecked? Dr. Evans told us that at the time Jesus lived the concept of the afterlife was undeveloped, a resting place, like an underground shroud, and it was not until the maturing of a religion one hundred years later when the fourth Gospel was written that Jesus said, "I am the resurrection and the life," and the belief in everlasting life in heaven, also known as salvation, became important. In earlier chapters we have seen the pitfalls in any belief that good works can guarantee a good life on earth. I suppose one could properly call any religion having such a belief immature. I submit it is equally immature to look to salvation in the afterlife as the reward for your good works in this life or as the reward for the steadfastness of your faith in Scripture in this life. The first translates into a bought paradise—do good or go to hell. The second translates into a subtler purchase based on merit.

Earlier, in asking why did Jesus die, I dismissed the answer of the resurrection as harmless and irrelevant to my discussion. Now I'm not so sure it is harmless. At times I fear it prompts people to forget that virtue is its own reward and to give up on this world prematurely. The first page of this book showed the thin line between survival and nonsurvival. Survival is made possible by hope and by fear, hope of an unexpected good day tomorrow, fear of the unknown afterlife upon death. You don't risk the fear so you must play the hope, and Jesus shows us how. If we seek a better world in this life and praise and thank God for all the blessings of living in this world and for the power of his grace during the travails, then, as Jesus indicated, God will take care of the rest.

My complaint with the salvation boys is that they play both sides of the street and so concern themselves with God's sphere to the detriment of their own. They remind me of the little boy who was found hugging himself in the corner of the room. When asked what he was doing, he replied; "I worked out and became strong. Now I am hugging myself so as not to lose any of my strength." This is my view of the eschatologists: off in the corner hugging themselves so as not to lose their exclusive predestined everlasting salvation. For most of us, the troops, the best preparation for the next campsite is to clean up the present campsite. This book shows how to leave this world a better place for having passed through it. Hence eschatology has for this book no more relevance than scatology, which curiously, in its own little way, is a study of another type of last things, and I shall leave this cathartic diversion with that.

I think the writing of this book has added to my understanding of myself. At the start I thought I was a pretty good Christian and a poor democrat. Now I find I may be a poor Christian (of the four great themes in the Old Testament—law, covenant, election, and salvation—I've just trashed two) but a better democrat. I look in the mirror and ask myself: could I voluntarily work for philosophical anarchy, try not to abuse another, push him down, use him as a stepping-stone for my own aggrandizement, try not to sell him what he does not need or want, try to work for the reduction of all taxes yet pay those that are due, try to help others gain a good education, try to work for the transformation of the church yet tithe in the process, take care of my own needs and at the same time try to feed the hungry, heal the sick, shelter and clothe the poor, and try to use my talents, fiscal and nonfiscal, for these endeavors? You know the alternative endeavors, such as going places, acquiring things, and other indulgences in excess of those permitted in the name of necessary recreation, other indulgences including the seven venial vices and much ado about nothing. Still looking in the mirror, I answer: I can do better. But the important question comes next. Do I believe my fellowman is capable of doing as I? Without hesitation the answer is yes. This is the absolute belief of the philosophical anarchist. This is what self-government is all about. This is the ideal of democracy. When everyone is able to take care of all his own needs the society has achieved self-government. No other government is necessary. What Plato called democracy and properly found to be unbearable is populism.

You may dislike this attempt of mine to appropriate the word *democracy* for my cause, so I shall make no further attempt to. By way of justification I would point out that the proper word for my concept of self-government is *autocracy* and the members of such a society would all be called autocrats. *Autocracy* comes from *auto,* meaning "self," and *cracy,* meaning "rule." Unfortunately, the word *autocracy* has been preempted by those who think in terms of an ideal individual ruler. They call the good ruler an aristocrat, which means rule of the best, or a benevolent despot, which means a well-wishing lord, and the bad ruler a tyrant, which comes from an old word meaning "lord," or an autocrat, in the sense that one strong self rules everybody. I shall continue, however, to talk in terms of philosophical anarchy as the political philosophers first introduced the concept to me. I shall not, however, give up religious support for the concept, as we shall now see.

Since the beginning of time even unto our own day, people have always irresponsibly longed for a strong and just ruler. Plato thought the answer to man's problems would be the rule of an aristocratic philosopher king. Dante's hope was for the world rule of a great, just, and holy emperor. Today people spend most of whatever political aspect their life holds in either building up their rulers or tearing them down, always wishing for a perfect one. If you won't accept this observation from me or from our contemporary politicians, please go and get it straight from the horse's mouth in I Samuel 8.

By the way, this yearning for a good ruler is the corollary of man's squealing: why did God make such an imperfect world and why does God allow such awful things to happen? Both of these follies—the yearning and the squealing—should disappear the moment one stops and thinks about it. An all-everything God—and surely you would not want your God to be less than omnipotent, omniscient, omnipresent, et cetera., et cetera—does not merely create a perfect man, rather, he creates one who has the potential to work toward his own perfection.

Let us now look at how Jesus handled the crowd's yearning for a messiah. Historians enjoy describing how during revolutionary periods a lifetime of happenings may be compressed into a period of a few days. Thus in one week Jesus went public and political, used force, and died. (This succinct sentence came out of a brilliant Palm Sunday guest sermon at my church several years ago.) If there is any worldly meaning to be found in Jesus' revolutionary week and its botched kingship, it has to be that he meant to lay to rest forever mankind's eternally dreaming of and wishing for wise and just rulers and good governments. And the churchman is every bit as guilty as the intellectual in his yearning for a good ruler. Within hours after Judas had Jesus killed because he was turning out not to be a kingly messiah, what happened? His disciples began laying the groundwork for his second coming (no matter where), and even today so-called theologians still continue to tinker with God's side of the equation that ties man to God, making no attempt to understand the meaning of the above-mentioned passage from Samuel or the story of the third temptation. What do they want, a second crucifixion?

This meaning of the crucifixion, I realize, is expressed as a negative witness. Before I can express it positively, I need to lay a foundation, which has two aspects. I have to describe what is wrong with the church in our country today and why I am permitted to point this out.

First, stated arbitrarily for ease of understanding, although probably incorrectly, as the truth often lies in-between, there are two ways the major denominations of the church in our country today view the world. The starting point for both ways is that, generally speaking, the world is bad. One group believes the church should have nothing to do with this bad world; the other group believes the church can and should try to make this mostly bad world better. I have no quarrel with either position. I do not know what the position of God is in the matter. I believe Scripture shows support for both positions coming from Jesus. My problem is that my mind tells me that the church today is not implementing either position logically.

On the one hand, the churchmen who believe the world is a hopeless case are offering me a long-suffering, sacrificial, pietistic message smacking of clericalism and privatism devoid of public relevance, a message whose alleged purpose is to prepare me for everlasting life, an insipid message that leaves me cold. I respectfully submit: everlasting life has inspirational meaning only when orchestrated together with everlasting damnation. Let's hear from this group some good old two-hour hellfire and brimstone sermons. For starters, I suggest this topic: "AIDS, the New Sodom."

On the other hand, the churchmen who believe they should transform the world start off every time using worldly methods, the very means Jesus rejected, and their failure every time is as assured as was the repeal of prohibition. I purposely set myself up for their screams to this sentence: "What methods does he think we have available to us other than worldly methods?" My answer: "God's methods." Now I must justify saying this.

As a lawyer I know one is not supposed to publish an article on a legal issue without digesting prior articles on the issue. Hence it is about time that I now finally have gotten around to reading Machiavelli, the world's resident expert on serpentine wisdom. I recommend him. He writes good universal stuff. One should remember he was a government functionary whose book, *The Prince,* was really a job application to a worldly ruler giving him policy advice. For this reason it should be read as fine advice for the leaders of our mandatory government to reflect upon, mindful that in general just the opposite advice would be appropriate for the leaders of our voluntary community. I owe to him two new insights: one negative, the other positive.

The negative insight is that he brought into focus a standard to be used in the mandatory community for determining what is necessary. You will remember I had no trouble in determining a standard for the voluntary community, which is to follow the right as Jesus shows it. Machiavelli's standard for the worldly ruler is to do what the temper of the times requires. Act cautiously in cautious times, boldly in bold times, for times change in a way rulers cannot control, and a ruler out of touch with the times will destroy himself and his people.

The positive insight that indirectly Machiavelli has given me is what enables me to criticize the church. This man was a serpent when it came to firming up worldly rulers. I liked the way he dismissed the law, to wit: "The chief foundations on which all states rest . . . are good laws and good arms. And since there cannot be good laws where there are not good arms, and where there are good arms there are bound to be good laws, I shall set aside the topic of laws and talk about arms."

But Machiavelli was chicken when it came to the church. Of the ecclesiastical states he wrote: "These then are the only safe and happy governments. But since they are ruled by a heavenly providence to which human reason cannot reach, I shall say nothing of them. Instituted as they are by God, and sustained by him, it would be a rash and imprudent man who ventured to discuss them."

I realize that maybe Machiavelli was being diplomatic, as he hoped to get a job from the pope's brother. But this thought of Machiavelli's has been held by many great scholars whose intellectual endeavors never mention God, as though never the twain should meet. As I have rejected Machiavelli's advice, I must confront his thought. I go back to the original source. The first serpent successfully tempted Eve with the promise of a godship. So these great scholars aren't going to get caught biting that apple.

I see it differently. I don't want to compete with God or even to cooperate with him. He does not need me. I need him. All I want to do is follow his will. I just cannot believe that on the one hand he gave me a mind, for which I shall always be grateful, and on the other hand he does not want me to use it in trying to understand him and his will for me. Although I cannot prove God, nothing in my belief about him is inconsistent with reason. Especially I cannot believe he wants me to keep him out of all my thought for a better world, because I believe that is what Jesus is all about. That is why I criticized both aspects of the church's attempt to follow Jesus today and that is why now I shall present what I believe to be the positive witness evidenced by Jesus' messianic failure.

My daddy done told me, "Son, fear not. There is no serpent. Only God and human nature. And human nature is sometimes good, sometimes bad." So it is fine and proper for Machiavelli to advise the princely ruler of a mandatory community ever to act mindful that all men are bad. Such a leader should always be prepared for the worst. Correspondingly, a leader of a voluntary community must believe man is capable of goodness or such a community will collapse. The negative witness of Jesus' death was that God refused to rule man. The positive witness is that what God has refused to do let no mere man presume to do. If God won't push me around, how dare you? And the minute you dare to, you are following the way of man, not the way of God.

Stated boldly, there is something that can be in each of us crying for voluntary obedience to the law of God and for government of self by self. To deny the possibility of everyone's being able to follow the will of God and to govern himself is to deny the possibility of God. What this something is, is God's concern. It is sufficient for me to think of it as conscience, knowledge with another, not God in me but, faithfully and hopefully, the grace and power of an outside person, the holy spirit. Logically, of course, man cannot follow the will of God, but with God all things are possible, so, remembering the Bull's caveat, let's cut it at that. Edward "the Bull" Warren was our professor of law who spent half the term studying just one case with his Socratic questioning of individuals until his final question of the class: "Gentlemen, do you agree that further discussion of this case, like discussions of the virgin birth, would end in final futility?"

So I say to the first group of churchmen: focus on the world before you; and to the second group: transform the world God's way; and to both groups: for Christ's sake, let's get on with it.

During my recent intermission from writing I also have read the two latest books on my subject that have come out of a great university. I saw them mentioned in a news item at the time of the 350th anniversary. One was on religion, the other on political philosophy. The former was brilliantly cosmetic; the latter, boringly brilliant. This I say not by way of disparagement—they are both good books—but in order to dramatize the need of religious support for philosophical anarchy. Logic without faith is not motivational. You need emotion to move. Faith can make the superficial seem brilliant, and brilliant logic can be a bore.

So I say to the philosophical anarchist: Take a bite of the apple—it's free, having been paid for dearly by mankind—don't be afraid to study God, because you are on his side and he can help you. Meanwhile your faith need only be that your goal is attainable in the way man attains goals, just as in graphing certain algebraic equations a curve gradually gets closer and closer to the line representing zero but never reaches it until infinity.

Let us conclude this chapter with the obvious: lack of faith in the achievement of philosophical anarchy following the will of God is the first exit off our highway to this kind of kingdom.

Chapter XI
More about Mandatory Communities

We have assumed that for survival man has three types of needs, physical, mental, and spiritual; each man should try to fulfill these needs for himself; and, to the extent that he cannot, others should help as needed, first family, then voluntary community, and, as a last resort, government. The reason for these assumptions is that, as all government is restraint, we are trying to keep restraints as self-imposed as possible so that under God each of us can be master of his own destiny. When the condition of self-restraint becomes so universal that the spirit of each and every one of us completely follows the will of God we will have reached utopia.

Note, therefore, that there is no such thing as a utopian form of government, as idealistically, governments should be unnecessary. It has been in this sense that I have used the term *philosophical anarchy*. By it I indicate a dispensing with external government only when everybody has developed the wisdom, the detachment, and the self-control of a philosopher, as internal restraint we must always have. Philosophical anarchy has nothing to do with the anarchy of the anarchists, terrorists, revolutionaries, or nihilists, to all of whom I would give as short shrift as Machiavelli would give to the children of a defeated hereditary king.

Understandably, therefore, I do not propose in this chapter to describe an ideal government for our country, nor even to offer professional blueprints for reducing present governmental activities in handling the needs of our people. The purpose of this chapter is to relight the way to the kingdom. I will be pointing out attitudes that cause us to lose the way. I will be looking at unsightly aspects of current life to see whether unnecessary government is lurking in the background. I will be talking only about physical needs, as I have described how the voluntary community can meet man's mental and spiritual needs. I will be making suggestions selected at random for lessening governmental involvement. One such way is to have private companies take over businesses the government is presently operating. Another way is for marketplaces presently regulated by government to take over this function and keep themselves clean. Still another way is through termination of unnecessary governmental supports, whether through direct subsidies or discriminatory favorable tax treatment. Appropriately, therefore, this chapter's first exit off the highway to the kingdom, exit #2, is reserved for those who in tackling any problem of human need do not first make every effort to solve it without invoking government.

I am told I cannot live for more than four days without water. In Philadelphia the city government controls the water system. I doubt I could find potable public drinking water not similarly controlled within four days' walking distance. So my most elemental need is now handled by the institution of last resort. Can one visualize a practical alternative? In what the political philosophers might call the state of nature, one can visualize man as a higher type of animal drinking running mountain stream water, what the canoeist would call at least Class III rapids. Such water would be safe only if the number of men and animals were exceedingly small. I read today that in my lifetime the population of the world has risen from just over 1 billion to 5 billion. Ergo, I am not able alone to handle my water-drinking problem.

Another alternative is the solution that was in effect in a town of about a hundred thousand people just before I moved there as a child. The water company was privately owned. Such an alternative is practical. It worked. The problem was that in the perception of the people it was unfair for man to make money selling water to his fellow-man. So rather than have government merely regulate the rate and the health factors, government took over the entire job under the ungodly pretext that the people owned the water, so no individual should. We cannot dismiss this perception that a private water company is unfair without deciding where we stand on several important concepts: the ownership of property, the corporation, the creation of monopolies, and the rate structure for monopolies.

With respect to the ownership of real property, that is, land and improvements thereto, I believe God owns the land and the raw materials. The institutional framework of society, however, should encompass private ownership of real and personal property in the nature of a stewardship to the extent necessary for the physical needs of each man. Philosophical anarchy demands that each man govern himself. Hence the fewer interrelationships with respect to the fulfilling of physical needs the better, as in every such relationship there will always be the thought that one is profiting from or abusing another. For that reason ownership of one's home is preferable to renting. It makes for more responsibility. Restraints, at first mandatory and later voluntary, on unreasonably large accumulations of property, especially land, may be necessary. Conceivably at first a land tax and later a voluntary contribution might discourage such unreasonable accumulations. In any event, I see no objection to a private water company's acquiring water properties or to each man's buying his own home and whatever property he needs for the operation of his business.

Our next concern is who is to own the private water company. If one were willing merely to have a group of people join together and operate the water company as though they were one individual, there would be no problem. The problem arises from the cultural factors that within comparatively recent times prompted the statutory creation of an artificial person known as the corporation. This artificial person separates the owners of the corporation from those who deal with it so that the owners are not responsible for what the corporation does. More precisely, the corporation is responsible only to the extent of the assets of the corporation. The justifications for the concept are primarily that this is the only way to raise the large amounts of capital required by these businesses and the only way to keep them operating efficiently in the public interest at all times. It allows many people to become owners without their participating significantly in or without their being responsible for the management. Moreover, as the owners elect directors who appoint the manager, the business runs smoothly upon the death of the owners, whose interest in the corporation merely passes to their legatees. It is fair to say that many owners of shares in a large corporation have no more knowledge or control of or responsibility for what their corporation does than I have for what my municipal water company does. Such shirking of responsibility for one's actions is the third exit off the highway to philosophical anarchy. The repeal of the concept of the corporation must occur before our water company can go private. The problem of centralization and continuity of management can be provided for as conditions to the grant of the monopoly. The problem of raising necessary capital funds can be handled by insurance covering the unlimited liability of the owner-operators, the cost of which would be borne by the consumers in the rate structure. Do not think for a moment these costs are not passed on to the consuming taxpayer in the case of the self-insuring municipal water company. The amount of capital necessary can be lessened by keeping the water service area small.

We must next decide whether or not to let our private water company have a monopoly. Arguments in favor of a monopoly are that it would be impractical, wasteful, and too costly to have competitive sets of water pipes throughout the city and that one company is more easily regulated than many. The main persuasive argument against having a monopoly is that it artificially prevents the law of supply and demand from fixing a fair price in the marketplace and thereby enables private entrepreneurs to gouge the public. Unless I can eliminate the need for water pipes altogether, I must reluctantly decide to have a monopoly in order to avoid multiple pipe systems.

A friend of ours of conservational bent and adequate means has installed in her summer home a dry sewage system in which all excrement drops into a basement vault and after five years may be taken out for use as fertilizer, the liquid having safely leaked into the ground in the meantime. Such a system saves a lot of water. Following the adage "if it's yellow let it mellow; if it's brown flush it down" saves a lot less. As there is so little pure water available today, maybe water should be bottled and sold like milk. Yesteryears' talk of giving milk companies monopolies fortunately remained just talk. Should I suggest that we now abolish all grants of monopoly for water companies and that we substitute bottled water for pipe-supplied water? Or should I suggest that bottled water be at least used for all residential purposes—drinking, bathing, dishwashing, laundry, and lawns? Then I thought of other monopolies. What about electric utilities, for example? I know so little about electricity. I once asked an electrical engineer to tell me what electricity is. After a lengthy discussion, he concluded not only that he could not tell me, but also that nobody knows what it is.

Wearily pondering these questions, I gleaned a new insight about seeking the kingdom, namely: When I look for the time when each man will govern himself, I am thinking of self-restraint and of self-reliance under God but not of self-sufficiency or of self-righteousness. Although with the utopian demise of external government, I, autocrat that I am, will finally enjoy the freedom of the tiger, as to all else I shall always remain a reluctant monkey. Said differently, when I write about man's being able to fulfill his own physical needs, I do not mean that he makes his own electricity if he knows how to or else goes without. All I mean is that each person pays his own way in fulfilling his own physical needs rather than look to government or to others to do it for him. There is no primitivism in this concept. The more advanced is our technology, the better it is for us. There also is no self-sufficiency in this concept. When I write about man relying upon himself in deciding what is the right way to handle life's problems, I mean that he acts on his own knowledge, and when knowledge is lacking and action is required before knowledge can be, he goes along with the suggestions of the decision makers in the community. There is no element of self-righteousness in this concept.

Let me dramatize the enormity of the task required by this last concept. Recently a scientist expressed to me concern about two entirely separate, potentially frighteningly devastating current developments about which I know nothing: something about genetic splicing and something about the Antarctic ozone hole in the stratosphere. Knowing nothing, where do I stand? What should be done and by whom? Following my thesis it will ultimately be the pope who offers the suggestions, that is, in the likely absence of total agreement of a completely knowledgeable world community. I do not develop this theme at this time, however, because although it probably would not take the pope long to tool up on genetic splicing, I am not at all sure, mindful of Galileo, that even today the pope would be prepared to speak authoritatively on the sun and the earth, as to which goes round which, let alone on the ozone hole. I know I could not.

My conclusion from this deeper insight, therefore, is that we all must learn more about everything. I hesitate to say everything about everything in view of the condition our two types of intellectuals are in now. According to current wit, the generalist daily knows less and less about more and more until finally he knows nothing about everything and the specialist knows more and more about less and less until finally he knows everything about nothing. It comes as no surprise, therefore, that our fourth exit is for the lazy. Meanwhile, where does all of this leave our unanswered questions about monopolies, genetic splicing, and the ozone hole? Mandatory government should now do what is necessary at the appropriate government levels. The ozone problem could be the subject of international treaties within and/or without the structure of the United Nations. Problems arising out of genetic splicing probably should be handled at the federal level of government, and with a few exceptions, such as rail and air travel and communications, grants of monopoly could be made at state and local levels.

Our next concern, now that we have granted the private water company a monopoly, is what government does to protect the people from being subjected to unfair rates. Let us put the problem in perspective. The company is entitled to a fair rate of return on its investment. Its investment includes the value of its assets. The value of its assets is determined by capitalizing the rate of return they produce. This rate of return is not knowable without first knowing what rates the public will pay. What these rates are to be is the question that started us on this circuitous path. So the water company has its experts' report conclude after pages of gobbledygook that in their expert opinion $X is a fair rate, a rate that the company arbitrarily picked out of the hat as the highest they could impose upon the people. Nonsense, reply both God and Caesar to such talk from those who oppress the people, and so we reserve the fifth exit on the road to the kingdom for those who complicate matters.

The solution is simple. Let the owner-operators have a reasonable salary commensurate with their actual work and their actual responsibilities and a reasonable return on the amount of money they actually reasonably invest in the business based upon market rates for the risk involved. Let government arbitrarily determine what is a reasonable amount in each case. Let the governmental regulatory costs be collected by means of a proportionate surcharge on each water bill, and let no one work for government who works for the water company, including family members or business associates.

Admittedly, such regulation will not be as easy or as simple as I have made it sound, but it is workable. Admittedly, there is a vast area between what is reasonably high and what is reasonably low. But the reasonableness of salary and of return can be tested against their counterparts in the general marketplace. With respect to the reasonableness of the amount of the investment of the company, particularly the investment in the land and water properties, we may expect to see continuations of current entrepreneurial practices of cheap purchases of such properties by strawmen or middlemen and of high-priced sales to the water company with insiders pocketing the difference. Jefferson's two foremost necessary evils, however, the government and the press, should be working together against this practice, and as the people become more educated and responsible the practice should run against the temper of the times. Meanwhile the government remains in the strong position of being able in the event of dereliction of duty or fraud on the part of the water company to revoke the monopoly and temporarily take over the company and operate it until appropriate private ownership and management can be found.

Comparable to my fear of unfair rates gouging the people is my fear of the contrary, the authorization of rates too low to ensure satisfactory water for the public. I can hear politicians campaigning for office on the promise to lower the water rates, and I can see the people jumping on this bandwagon. Quite frankly, I do not know how to handle this. I do not like the obvious groveling counteraction of letting the water companies have lobbyists and letting the companies support their own candidates. Any expense of theirs is so doing is certainly not to be included as an expense in determining the rate structure.

I now have the task of coming up with an alternative solution, which means I have to think. There are two ways of thinking: doing it on your own or taking the thoughts of others. The advantage of reading while writing is that it stimulates the thought process. The disadvantage is that it may prevent you from thinking for yourself or from expressing in your own fashion an idea that is crystallizing in your mind at the time you come upon it in refined state in the writing of another. In an early chapter you will remember I pointed out that this was not to be the book of a scholar. Everything was to be subordinated to my mission of sending the message to the world that the kingdom of God and the anarchical utopia of the philosopher are the same idea and of sending to churchman and scholar alike the challenge to get on with its realization. I believe all history points in this direction, although I am not aware of the two concepts having been linked before. Hence I said I was going to make no attempt to reinvent the wheel but rather to use it wheresoever I found it by taking help from the relevant thinking of others. I added that in fairness I would try to indicate along the way when I remembered a thought as not having been my own.

In this vein you should know I read Machiavelli's *The Prince* in a Norton Critical Edition translated and edited by Robert M. Adams and published in 1977 together with backgrounds and criticism. I read it as Machiavelli read books following the advice of Dante, by jotting down notes, as otherwise you cannot remember what you read, and it gave me a delightfully full wheel. The wheel culminates with Adams's own exhortation for freedom of thought in an open and free marketplace of ideas, a freedom that, fortunately, we already have in our country, if only we can keep it. There follow several tidbits from this book that I am using as wheels.

My above-mentioned two ways of thinking come from Livy, who as quoted by Machiavelli described the three types of brains as those that think for themselves, those that understand from others, and those that do neither.

Adams deplores our present electoral process, as the candidates have two faces: when running for election they are virtue personified, all things to all men; when elected they are as devious as lawyers (most are) in passing complicated laws with concealed loopholes for the special interests whose money elected them.

Machiavelli, noting that Plato's five different forms of government each contained the makings of its own destruction, suggested that all of these five forms ought to be embraced in one government, a government composed of prince, nobles, and people, so that they could check and balance each other. That Machiavelli's concept may have been the origin of our present three-branch system is my own thought.

Now let us return to my task of containing the power of demagogic politicians in order to ensure fair rates for our water company. For years now I have deplored the lack of class in our society. I use this word, *class,* in its slang usage, to indicate excellence and character. No presidential candidate has captured my imagination since Bob Taft, and even he held wrong ideas and came from the wrong school. Imagine what I think of most of the lesser candidates. Sometimes I feel that to achieve greatness in our contemporary society one must be either cunning at best or deceitful at worst. Is this all wholly the fault of the people? Could this not partially be the fault of the system? Here is a suggestion. Let us combine the above thought of Machiavelli with that of Hamilton, the founding father whose thinking I most admire, and have a certain number of the U.S. Senate elected for life on good behavior. Let us say up to one-third of that body but never enough to be able alone or in collusion with the executive to amend the constitution. The people could elect these lifetime senators as they do the president, and they should be elected from candidates selected by the senate from those of its then membership who have at least begun their second six-year term. Would this encourage more high-caliber people to enter politics? Would this create another check against the mediocre extremes of democracy? Could not such a group, secure in their jobs, more responsibly stand up against a foolish policy of a popular president? We are a long ways from our kingdom. Perhaps such a change is necessary in the meantime. After all, *people* and the *poplar* tree come from the same Latin word *populus,* the latter because its petiole slants differently from that of other trees so that like one of its species, the quaking aspen, its leaves bend with the wind. If my thought is feasible on the federal level, it could equally apply on the local level so that a group of respected elders could tell the municipality that was considering not allowing the water company to charge a fair rate, "You just do not do that."

That last statement certainly sounds haughty. Do I really mean it? These so-called respected elders could make the same haughty put-down of a good suggestion emanating in the legislature. Didn't we fight the American revolution to get rid of just such haughty nobility? Isn't this a step backward? Here, as always in dealing with problems of the mandatory government, one must take a balanced approach. I conclude that the scales tilt in favor of giving our society a little nobility. I am aware, however, that when one in authority summarily tells another what he may not do he smothers the other's spirit. So I have no objection if you think I have just trapped myself into taking the sixth exit off the highway to the kingdom, the exit reserved for those who intimidate and whose sin of intellectual pride is one of the most deadly ones.

Our last tidbit concerning Machiavelli is a quotation from Francis Bacon, who associated Machiavelli with the serpentine wisdom of the Bible. Just a few pages ago I did, believing myself to be the first to do this. Wrote Bacon: "We are much beholden to Machiavelli and other writers of that class, who . . . describe what men do . . . For it is not possible to join the wisdom of the serpent with the innocence of the dove, except men be perfectly acquainted with the nature of evil itself . . ."

Anybody with perspicacity like that, little wonder some say he wrote Shakespeare! This quotation compels me to set forth my credentials in evil. I believe enough time has passed so that I may now finally reveal, both decently and legally, this hitherto secret story, especially as this enables me to tell it my way before the media make up their own story. I held only four full-time jobs in my life, three of which were given me by graduates of the wrong school. All four employers were sterling men, whose influence crops up in this book. By now it is obvious that I use *wrong* in the expression *the wrong school* in a secondary sort of way. At my school when one does something wrong he really boots it all the way. Witness this boot:

Upon graduating from law school and passing the bar exams in the summer of 1941, I hitchhiked to the national capital to find civilian work of national importance, having failed to obtain such employment with the FBI, whose application form developed for their files the fact that I would not fight in any war. I promptly found work in the then equivalent of the Central Intelligence Agency. It was a night job typing up all the secret messages that our reader brought to two of us early each evening in decoded manuscript form from the State Department, which had received them that day from its listening posts throughout the world. Once typed, these messages were then ready for the use of our regional experts the next day. It was not until the following spring that the record finally caught up with me, whether through security clearance of the FBI or through draft boards I do not know. So for nearly three months before Pearl Harbor I read cable after cable containing rumor after rumor that Japan would attack the next weekend. In doing so I came to like the messages from one of our consuls as he spoke with authority. Midweek before Pearl Harbor his message was that a dependable local official of a foreign government, quoting an unnamed source always proven reliable in the past, told him this was to be the weekend. Sunday afternoon I came out of the Washington movie house at about three o'clock to face the newspapers' black headlines without surprise.

What did I then and what do I now make of this? If I had been at the appropriate post to receive that message I would have got it in timely fashion into the hands of the next appropriate superior receiver, and if I had been such next receiver I would have got it in timely fashion into the hands of the next, and so on until it reached the top and all the ships at sea. It was the great boot of my age, whether through grossest negligence or grossest incompetence at some point in the chain or through—you say it. I am not going to complete this customary form of legal allegation. Nor am I going to try to surmise why shortly thereafter the authoritative consul was kicked upstairs to a higher post in South America.

Machiavelli told his prince (meaning "ruler or king") that he must always be courageous, bold to act, prepared to enter war on his own timetable and not on that of the enemy, that he cannot remain neutral when others are fighting because both sides will despise him and the winner after winning will take him on alone, and he must always be prepared, even at the risk of appearing to be cruel, to cause the death of a few if it can advance his position. Following the same process of thought, our prince had been helping England for years. He knew England alone could not hold off Hitler. He believed we would have to fight Hitler at some time, but he had strong opposition at home to our entering the war. What timetable could be more appropriate for galvanizing the people into fighting unity than to allow a sneak attack to take place and a day of infamy to happen? And at what proportionately little cost?

I do not know what to make of all this now, nor did I then. I trust no reader will reach any conclusion without studying the historical sources, rather than using the insight of a mere night typist, especially one who violated at the time and who has ever after encouraged his own secretaries to violate the secretary's first commandment: thou shalt never make any attempt to understand what you are typing. For obvious reasons I made no simultaneous prick of the pen at the time this all was happening, and I am just now getting around to documenting my story nearly fifty years later, as tardy as the evangelists were in documenting their story. The serpentine insight is that I feel confident my story has lost nothing in its writing and I believe it has also gained nothing, but of this I am not confident. Perhaps the evangelists felt likewise.

But this I do know. Much can be done in the name of a balanced approach, but when what appears to be necessary (the "not to be") jeopardizes my "to be" itself, then the scales become meaningless and I escape to my God every time. Machiavelli is great for understanding, especially for understanding, alone among those who have written about government, that government is not an engine for morality, as the essence of government is and always has been bad. This is why Machiavelli still lives. But Machiavelli is not good for following. His way is not God's way or mine. Reader, do you think Francis Bacon would give me a passing grade in his course on the knowledge of the nature of evil so that I might be given a dispensation to go back to work on the road to the kingdom?

After water our next physical necessity is food. I will look to the marketplace to determine all aspects of the production of food—amount, quality, variety, et cetera—except for the necessary regulations by the Food and Drug Administration of the health aspects. Farmers will own their farms and produce what they can sell. Having abolished the concept of the corporation, I would expect to see few large holdings, but any economic oppression therefrom can be regulated. Necessary benefits customarily attributable to large-scale farming can be obtained through cooperatives, with insurance protection as required. Comparable cooperatives can handle overproduction problems with voluntarily accepted quotas, although conceivably mandatory quotas may initially be necessary. Crop failures from natural causes should pose most underproduction problems, and farmers would look first to their own savings and next to borrowings to tide them through until the next crop can be harvested. If all else fails, they may have to train for and find other work. This now is a fit place to talk about the investment of savings.

It would be simpler if, like the proverbial sparrow, man worked each day just enough, but no more than enough, to meet what it costs him to live that day. It is nice that man has the option of working daily both for his daily bread and to save for a time he need not work. I suppose, if there is a good reason, it is all right for a man to borrow to live today with the intention of working tomorrow to meet both daily needs and loan repayments. At any rate, our current system contemplates investment in others of what one makes in excess of what one spends. Such investment primarily takes two forms: loans to others to be repaid within a certain time together with interest at a rate commensurate with the risk involved of no repayment; or purchases from others of a specified share of the ownership of their business property together with a specified share of the earnings of their business. Conceptually, I find no fault with either form, whether debt or equity investment. For example, in discussing private property I mentioned the desirability of residential home ownership. Real estate mortgage lending would appear to be the only practical way to finance such ownership. A residence is not income-producing, so equity investment is not feasible. In general, equity investment is preferable to investment in debt, however, for the same reasons Polonius advised his son, "Neither a borrower nor a lender be." When you buy a share of ownership you assume responsibility (as we are abolishing limited liability), accept the risks, and reap the rewards. When you make a loan to another, generally, you fail to appreciate the risks and you shirk responsibility. Regulation, therefore, should not give special beneficial treatment to lending, and if financial cartels become too powerful, regulation may even have to restrict lending.

Let us now set the stage for delving into investments and the financial markets. We will now be in the midst of excrement, pyramids of hazardous excrement. Following Orwell's advice to use short words, which in this case are unavoidably ugly, I call it "big shit." I broke into this game by attending seminars sponsored and taught by the brightest and the best in the country. I heard things like this:

"Now if your client wishes to try any of these questionable approaches, be sure to document the deal so thoroughly that by the time the regulators are able to read the thousand of pages, the time period within which they can sue your clients will have expired." Or things like this: "In this hundred-million-dollar disaster your client has walked away with 15 million; will his position be upheld? In answer, we will now hear from our panel. These eight experts will now give us the answers. I say answers because our panel has ten answers. You see, no two members of the panel could agree on any answer and two of the panel each had two different answers, as they could not even make up their own minds."

Can you call anybody dishonest or even a poor sport when you are working in such a league? Under such circumstances is regulation necessary? A wealthy financier once told me that if anyone wants to defraud him in this game there is no way he can stop him. If entrepreneurs with the best brains around and lifetimes of experience cannot prevent fraud against themselves, do you think regulators can prevent fraud against the public? Moreover, what often happens is that the bright young securities or tax lawyer or accountant starts up the ladder in the bureaucratic regulatory service in the hope that after he has acquired a sufficient amount of inside knowledge, by which I mean only knowledge of how the system works, he may be able to jump over to the side of the regulated and make the big bucks as adviser or consultant to the entrepreneurs. This then requires the regulators to become more sophisticated, to enact more regulations to plug up the loopholes, and to hire more and more regulators. The apparatus feeds upon itself like Aesop's oak tree that doubled in size at each blow of the woodsman's ax (hereinafter called Aesop's fable).

In common law gambling was not illegal. It was just ignored by government. Hence the expression *gentlemen honor their bets.* If you wanted to gamble you made sure you trusted the gentleman with whom you bet and any gentleman who was stakeholder, for if either welched you had no recourse. The attitude of the courts was: *volenti non fit inuria,* which is to say, to those willing there is no injury. (I find it amusing that those cold luncheon sandwiches that often I have picked out from between the piles of documents heaped high on the negotiating tables took their name from the eighteenth-century Earl of Sandwich because he took time thus to eat at the gambling tables.)

So here is my proposal. Let us not wait to see whether the private sector can take care of the problems arising in the securities marketplace. Let us immediately abolish the regulation of the security markets. The security players are too bright to be caught at reasonable expense. Theirs is a game where success goes to the brainiest, who ahead of the pack devises a new complicated gimmick so that the regulators either play a losing game of catch-up or just go fishing in frustration. If through luck they should hook into a big one, master deal maker that he is, he inveigles them into trading to him their hook and line with him attached in return for a net containing a few small fish and a few bucks.

By my suggestion to abolish the regulation of the securities laws I do not intend to abolish general law, civil procedures such as cases of common-law fraud, or criminal actions such as offenses of extortion, bribery, and fraud, which will remain helpful in catching the ordinary crook or the greedy entrepreneur when, in a rare case, he makes a flagrant mistake. In addition, the taxing of these financial enterprises is a different matter to be handled differently. The trick here is to pay no attention to their squeals for fair treatment. Taxes are not fair. They are necessary. Such squeals only lead to exception to exceptions to exceptions in the tax laws until your tax structure is so complicated that any saltworthy lawyer will be able to find at least one answer of the many possible answers to his client's tax situation that will enable the client to escape taxation. Continuing, the trick is to have a simple tax law that results in a rough sort of justice. When the entrepreneurs go into their intimidating stance, saying, "Our request for fairness requires only a very simple change; we really fail to see why you are unable to understand it," ask them to put it in writing at their own expense in answer to your carefully thought out oral questions. Then give their written reply to your attorney, who will not find it simple at all.

Is our society ready for the abolition of the regulation of the security markets? I doubt it. But because I think this is now feasible and because it shows the way to the kingdom, I am going to pursue it. I have no complaint, however, with the legalists who, believing justice is attainable under law, will disparage this approach of mine. These manipulations by which financial wizards using other people's money extract money from other financial wizards using other people's money are often so heinous that the people may insist on having regulators try to catch these manipulators. To them I say good luck, even though their pursuit increases my tax burdens and my living costs as I, as consumer, pay the cost to the producer of raising this capital. But I am not going to spend any of my time on this fruitless and unprincipled chase. Instead, in seeking a solution I now offer a substitute that may have consequences far better, far worse, somewhere in-between, or none of the above if not adopted.

A friend of mine, a Pennsylvania Dutchman, brought up in the Mennonite tradition, had just returned from a visit to his childhood farming community. One of his younger cousins had run afoul of the law, and my friend wanted to visit him in prison. He told me how on arrival he went into a large living room where many of the family were gathered and asked if anyone cared to come with him on his visit to the prison. He said to me, "There was no response. You could have heard a pin drop. Their faces were without expression, almost sullen. It really was quite scary." By now, reader, you realize they were shunning. Let us now talk about shunning, papal indexes, kangaroo courts, vigilante justice, boycotts, old boy and new boy networks, back scratching, private clubs, guilt by association, and blacklists, the type of stuff that may rush into the vacuum created by the departure of the law from any area. The method I will use is, first, to reduce the size of the vacuum, then to set up my substitute proposal, and finally to test it against these objectionable methods of handling man's relationships.

The financiers who play the game are always reluctant to take the great risks without plenty of insulation from personal liability and without using other people's money. So at the same time that we deregulate the securities market, we should do two other things:

1. We should abolish the concept of the corporation following our suggestion for the water company; and
2. We should abolish the bankruptcy laws. These laws are the last refuge of the ruthless, aggressive financiers, those whose lives are lived along the top of the fence

that separates the legal from the illegal. When occasionally, despite their brains, they fall off on the illegal side, they cry to Uncle for mercy and get a clean slate. These laws are a beautiful example of a misguided attempt to do good through force. They meet no test of necessity. Their abuse by debtors is matched only by the usurious abuse by creditors of compounding, high, default rates of interest. In even-handed treatment, therefore, at the same time we abolish the bankruptcy laws we will mandate a default rate of one-quarter of some prime rate but no higher than 3 percent per annum at simple interest upon any debtor's declaring himself insolvent, and during the period he remains so. Even today the voluntary community is sufficiently vigilant to be able to take on this responsibility of helping any industrious fallen debtor meet such limited obligation and get back over the fence.

Individual investors also can help discourage these ruthless financiers by not giving their chips to others, although we realize there will always be investors who do so in the hope of receiving, say, a 30 percent return rather than the 5 percent the banks pay, which is a rate that, admittedly, often does not match the rate of inflation.

My substitute proposal is that there be published for the investing public a blacklist on which appear the names of those financiers whose practices do not meet the smell test as determined by the financial community, a list that is to have no enforcement consequences. Its only effect is to give the individual investor the option of avoiding those whose practices are considered to be unacceptable. Could not the applicable trade association, whether an association of financial dealers, brokers, salesmen, or consultants or one of the financial exchanges, publish for public use a list of their individual members whose conduct has been questionable or, as an alternative, a list of those whose conduct has been acceptable? From such lists could not a master list be compiled by an appropriate master association? The costs of publishing these lists should be kept modest so that membership fees in the associations could cover them.

Now, before you laugh at such a ridiculous return to the historically primitive, uncivilized practice of blacklisting, let us review how we got there. In discussing governments, Machiavelli pointed out that he was not going to write about ideal governments like Plato and all the rest; he was going to write about the real thing. Similarily, I am writing about the way the law actually works. The securities marketplace is a mess. Its participants do not know what rules they are operating under. An overburdened bureaucracy, in trying to regulate the industry from many and often inconsistent approaches, even stoops to nitpicking and approving the form and the content of the documents that are being used. Sharp practices are rife. Regulation, although ideally necessary, realistically is costly and worthless. The only way regulation could possibly be effective would be to pay the regulators more than the regulated, because no one can play the game on either side without years of study and experience in finance, accounting, and law, years of time that no one is willing thus to spend without visions of ultimately receiving tremendous monetary rewards, but the public cannot afford to pay the necessary amount for such regulation.

For the legalist all of the above poses no problem; when the choice, as here, is between too much law and too little law, he viscerally sees too little law as anarchy, his ultimate abomination, and so chooses too much law. Trained as he is in the law, he knows he can transfer most of its burdens to the unlawyered people. The philosophical anarchist, however, has a problem here, especially since the voluntary community is not yet ready to accept the function of suggesting to the financiers how they should behave voluntarily. Can you image Rome today witnessing heinous offenses in its domain without trying to render the situation sacred, that is, without invoking sanctions? But the kingdom seeker can never accept the choice of too much law. He remembers how too much law killed even God (chapter 7). Fearlessly he must move on into this new territory and allow this marketplace to clean up its own act using as a standard what is known as generally accepted behavior.

Conceptually, I have contempt for such behavior as a standard. Like fair play, good faith, ethics, and morality, these unenforceable concepts are hitched to no absolute standard. Ethics and morality, for example, come from the respective Greek and Latin words both meaning "custom or habit," which in turn mean nothing more than "something you do regularly," like putting on your clothes daily, your costume or habit. All these concepts remind me of your gifted sports opponent who pontificates that it is not whether you win or lose that counts, it is how you play the game. Thus having shamed you into giving up your compensating craft, a moment later he springs upon you a little craft of his own, all the time smiling ever so graciously.

Although we shall move ahead fearlessly, we may not move ahead foolhardily. I can remember the day when doctors and lawyers were able to maintain the integrity of their professions through their professional associations reasonably well in a rough sort of way. Today's legalistic society has brought into prominent use the malpractice case as another means to achieve such professional integrity, but whether this is a step forward is dubious. Why? Again the answer is: because of what is happening to the other side in the continuing warfare between the law and the spirit. Too numerous are the fine young doctors, true healers, who are dropping out of the practice of medicine because malpractice insurance costs have become prohibitive. In such a situation the procedural way to the kingdom is to back up and start over. Let us now do so, using the financial markets as our example. These financial entrepreneurs are big boys. They do not need bureaucrats to tell them how to run their business. They know it is in their self-interest to keep their marketplace in reasonable order. It is not foolhardy to let them try. For this reason we give them the opportunity under the guidelines developed below from some of the pitfalls I see.

Preliminarily, we ought to look at those who can be expected to oppose our abolishing this regulation, in order to meet their objections as best we can. First will be the legalists, who will cry out, "You are destroying the law! By blacklisting you are depriving a man of his livelihood and his character without due process of law, and you could be the one blacklisted." To them I respond, "Not so. I am not destroying the law. I am merely pushing back an unwarranted intrusion. I have specifically provided that blacklisting is irrelevant in enforcement and licensing procedures. Blacklisting could not happen to me because I have no desire to play with other people's money. If you do, all I ask is that you maintain a good reputation in the community of those who do. As arbitration proceedings have obtained a limited acceptance in certain areas where legal procedures became excessively time-consuming and costly, so with your cooperation your fraternity ought to be able to promulgate fair blacklisting procedures."

The next objectors will be those investors who have been burnt and who may be burnt in the future in spite of the availability of blacklists. To them we politely point out that even though they assumed this risk, they continue to have the protection of the courts in fraud and other cases of this nature. Finally and surprisingly, we may expect to see objecting those prudent, timid financiers who in the exhausting competition with their more ruthless risk-taking brethren regularly ask government for a helping hand. To them we politely suggest either they share responsibility for keeping tidy the marketplace in which they earn their living or they find employment in another marketplace that is easier to keep clean.

The legislation taking the securities laws off the books will not tell the financial markets how to run their business or how to maintain the integrity of their marketplace. This legislation affirmatively will only require the publishing of the blacklists. In so doing it will grant immunity to those involved in the process from most criminal prosecution and from all civil suits such as those arising from slander, libel, defamation, and malicious interference with one's business. Most important, this legislation will prohibit all sanctions and the use of any self-help and will expressly give no enforcement powers to the associations. Hence fears of papal indexes, kangaroo courts, or vigilante justice are misguided. Blacklisting only puts the investing public on guard. Specifically, there is to be no connection between blacklisting and licensing procedures. Licensing procedures assure the public of the competence of the financier, not his morality. These procedures will continue to be administered by mandatory government until such time as the financial community can assume this responsibility. Indeed, it would be unjust and illegal if there were any connection between blacklisting and licensing, as those blacklisted were never given their day in court to demand that any complaints against them be proven. Hence blacklisting does not result in the loss of any professional license to do a financial business nor of the right to acquire any additional such licenses. In consequence, the one listed may not by reason of the listing be deprived of active membership in the trade associations, even in the listing association. So there is no activity comparable to shunning, boycotting, or maintaining a private club. The deregulatory legislation will not include foreign financial operations, because it would be foolhardy now to look to an international community that does not yet exist in community form.

I have taken unusual pains to show how the voluntary community might take over the supervision of the securities markets for two reasons:

1. As I have seen firsthand how some of this marketplace operates under regulation, I was emboldened to risk dispensing with such costly and ineffective mandatory government; and
2. As I believe most people do not belong in this marketplace, I was willing to allow its own voluntary community to take over this regulation even though our proposed universal voluntary community with its standard of righteousness under God is not sufficiently equipped now to do so.

If self-supervision should fail I would blame it upon my eagerness to get on with it. I do so love the pope and his goodness. I fail to understand why people do not readily follow his teachings or why he tries to force people to do so in countries where he is dominant. It is admittedly a slow process, but one day I hope he will have the time to understand the marketplace of securities as well as he understands the marketplace of sex so he can tell us how to play the former game as well as he now does the latter. Meanwhile let us plod ahead fearlessly, allowing the fearful to get off here at exit #7.

Let us first, however, refresh our memories of what we are doing. We are looking for ways in which governmental involvement in our daily lives may be lessened. We are using the farmer as the prototype of all workers and looking at how government affects his life. We saw that in years when his crops fail from natural causes we hope he will have savings to tide him over. We have just seen that the financial markets are a questionable place for workers to invest their savings. We also know that the governmental costs of regulating these markets that raise the capital for our producers are passed on to the workers either in the taxes they pay or in the prices they pay for their purchases. From the standpoint of both saving money and not losing what money he has, the farmer would be better off without financial markets and their regulation. So where should our farmer put his savings?

Many believe the safest investments today are the obligations of the federal government known as U.S. Treasury bonds, notes, and bills. But how safe are they? What is all this talk about a 3 trillion national debt? What does this mean? Is this another unsightly aspect of current life where unnecessary governmental activity is present? Why does the government need to borrow? It can tax. It can make money. I do not like the budget deficit. It contradicts my starting points, one of which is my dislike of borrowing. I believe individual saving is desirable. One is more responsible if he saves for his rainy days rather than looks to others for help as soon as the rains come. Conversely, individual borrowing is generally undesirable because, when troubles come, the borrower's credit standing disappears and he can look only to others for help. One can think of exceptions. A home mortgage, for example, probably encourages responsibility, especially if there has been a substantial down payment. The value of the house hopefully will always exceed the diminishing indebtedness. Another starting point is that, after one has a home, adequate money in the bank, and adequate insurance, individual savings are more appropriately invested in shares of the ownership of businesses than in loans to businesses or governments, because with ownership comes responsibility.

Let us pause for a moment to test these starting points. How can we advocate savings and not advocate borrowings? Don't we have to have a borrower for every lender who saves? Isn't it less risky to loan to others than to participate in ownership with others? These are fair questions, but their answers do not contradict our starting points. What their answers show is that in the marketplace there will be those who prefer to have their savings invested in loans rather than in ownership and there will be risk-taking spenders and entrepreneurs who prefer to borrow in excess of their assets. Legally, creditors have first claim on the assets of defaulting debtors. This is why historically lending has been considered less risky than ownership. But in total disasters, when the risk taker in bankruptcy pays back nothing on his borrowings, the individual or institution whose savings were invested in loans to such a risk taker will be able to appreciate the thoughts behind our starting points.

Is there any danger of the government of the United States being such a risk taker? Is there any danger of the government of the United States repudiating its debts? Why has our government let its debt become so large that

I even ask such questions? How did we get into this deficit-financing mess anyway? Here is how. In a pluralistic democracy many citizens refuse to vote for both those whose platform is to raise taxes to meet expenses and those whose platform is to reduce governmental programs. The compromise to keep the system working is for the government to borrow and increase the public debt. Politicians know they must give the people what they want today or they are politically dead tomorrow, so to hell with the day after the next, when the country goes bankrupt and, like a gutsy entrepreneur, cries for mercy, repudiates its debts, and gives itself a clean slate. The government would probably not use the repulsive word *repudiate.* It need only declare a short moratorium (extendable endlessly) during which no interest would accrue.

My point is not that I see any likelihood of this happening, though governments have been known to default on their debts, but that I see no need whatsoever in our government's taking this risk. The risk far outweighs any possible benefit. Though the likelihood of the risk occurring appears to be slight, the extent of the risk, if it did occur, is enormous. Query, whether a government could go bankrupt and survive, so great would be the loss of faith of the people and of the world in it. The situation differs from that of the individual bankrupt, who takes his clean slate to a place where his credit standing has not caught up with him. This devastating risk reeks of debtors' prisons of the common law in prebankruptcy times, of Siberian gulags for fallen rulers, and of violent upheavals during bloody revolutionary periods.

And what are the benefits that justify such risks? Governmental programs that we cannot afford, so we pass this multi-trillion-dollar burden and ever accumulating and compounding multibillion-dollar interest charges on to the next generations of our citizens. Some of these programs are not only unnecessary but also even impossible of fulfillment. Let me consider just two: universal health insurance and military defense. These two concerns arise from man's two greatest, insatiable fears: the unknown beyond and the strange outside, namely, death and foreigners. With today's medical advances there is not a doctor alive who will say there is enough money available to prolong the life of everyone as long as possible. There never has been a general who would say his forces of personnel and matériel were great enough to ensure the safety of his country. The futile attempt to achieve the benefit of just these two governmental programs merely fuels the risk, as in Aesop's fable. I contemplate the voluntary community's taking over health problems in steps comparable to those I have detailed for education. I contemplate the institution of a new world order as a method for eliminating the arms race. As a first step I have drafted a constitution for the world's consideration. Meanwhile all that is necessary for government to do about health is to balance the necessity of keeping an old fart like me alive against the righteousness of not breaking the spirit of tomorrow's kid; and all that is necessary for our government to do about defense is to keep one step ahead of the next guy while all the time opting for programs that foster a worldwide, open, free marketplace of ideas, products, and passage.

Let the politicians, therefore, cease being all things to all people and let them vote the funds for the programs they espouse. The people are going to have to pay for the programs eventually, so why not at the front end and thereby save the billions of dollars in interest charges?

Now that we have seen how we got into this mess, here are the three initiatives I would simultaneously begin to take in order to get us out of it:

1. Commence both processes for enacting an amendment to the constitution forbidding the government from borrowing or using its credit to borrow.
2. Commence a bipartisan reverse pork barrel approach toward a drastic reduction of governmental programs.
3. Commence congressional processes along bipartisan lines toward the enactment of legislation requiring future budgets to be balanced through tax revenues rather than through borrowings.

In order to double-check the validity of these proposals, I wish to tackle the budget deficit from several different angles. There follow:

1. Thoughts on why the money-making powers of the government are not fundamentally relevant to the issue.
2. Thoughts on why the fact that governmental borrowing can be used to shift unfairly the tax burden from certain groups of people to other groups is also not fundamentally relevant.
3. An analysis of governmental borrowing from the point of view of the lenders.

Let us, therefore, see why having the government make money is not the solution. First, it would not be a proper function of government to make money in the sense you and I do. There is no way that a governmental enterprise can operate in competition with a private enterprise on a fair, level playing field. How could the government fairly tax and regulate itself or share incentive profits among the political managers? If the government were to operate a business clothed with the public interest, such as mail delivery or railway transportation, which it now does, or such as telephone services or television broadcasting, which it now does not, such operation would not be for profit but because of necessity. Hopefully, the operation would break even and not require any subsidy. You will remember how the determination of whether the government should operate such a business might be made by looking back at our discussion of the municipal water company.

Secondly, with respect to seigniorage, the customary sense in which the government makes money, I would like to be able to leave to the experts what quantity of coins to mint, of paper money to print, and, more important, of credit to have outstanding. After all, how dare I talk about economics when I know so little? Unfortunately, the experts say that both fiscal policy and monetary policy are political problems. The moment a problem becomes a political problem in a democracy, I as one of the people am responsible for it and so I must grapple with it. I cannot pass this problem, as I did in 1976, to the leader who says, "Trust me," because it will turn out that he too did not understand monetary policy. So here is my thinking.

A productive economy is more important than a sound monetary policy, so in times when you cannot have both, the latter is the loser. As monetary decisions are entirely arbitrary and political and as economists think more like theologians or philosophers than like scientists, I would hope the Federal Reserve Board would continue to enjoy an independent autonomy as one of the necessary checks and balances in our system, comparable to the third branch of our government. My hunch is that if I were to study the economics involved I would find that fluctuations caused by the capriciousness of the money regulators could eventually be avoided by pegging by fiat the amount of outstanding money and credit to a fixed percentage of the gross national product, which today is about $4 trillion, and by allowing interest rates to fluctuate in a free and open marketplace. Consequently, I would hope the decisions of the experts with respect to the amount of outstanding money and credit would reflect what is necessary for exchange purposes and have a logical relationship with the amount of the gross national product.

When a government puts into circulation an excessive amount of money, it has the effect of reducing the worth of the dollars outstanding, whether in the hands of the rich or in the next paychecks of the workers, just as a corporation's issuance of additional shares of its stock dilutes the outstanding shares. When a corporation issues such additional shares to the public it asks for a quid pro quo in an amount that is favorably comparable to the then quoted value of the stock. Hence in a democracy the rich and the workers ought to be able to struggle together to see to it that the government does not abuse its money-making powers unless the excess funds are to be used for a program they approve. Even in this case the necessary funds would more properly come from taxation so that the people, in bearing directly the cost of the program, may more readily understand their responsibility for it. Incidentally, I detest our graduated tax on earned income. I believe any tax on earned income is a stumbling block to incentive and industry and, when graduated, such a tax becomes manifestly unfair. Generally, the harder one works the more one earns, but except in most cases of top management, such earnings increase at best only arithmetically and not geometrically, as do the federal income tax brackets. If asked I would suggest as an alternative a protection tax such as I have used in drafting a constitution for the world in chapter 8. The purpose of this chapter, however, is to show ways to reduce governmental activities rather than to show ways to improve the government of our country.

A reason many intelligent people, some shrewd and some innocent, wink at the borrowing binge of the demogogic politicians is that they believe the eventual costs can be shifted from themselves and their children to others. That borrowing can shift tax burdens unfairly is demonstrable. For example, suppose you are a public school director. You view your job as that of providing the best education for the children of your district at the lowest cost to their parents and the rest of the district through school taxes. Your annual payroll is $100x, so you collect taxes of $100x at the first of the year, deposit the $100x in the bank, receive the going interest rate of 6 percent at the end of the year, borrow during the year from or through the bank to meet the monthly payroll at 4 percent, as interest on school notes is exempt from federal income tax in the tax returns of the lenders, and start the next year $2x ahead for every $100, a surplusage that becomes dramatic when the prime becomes 20 percent. The abuse is that I and the other federal taxpayers who do not live in your school district must pay increased taxes to make this surplusage possible. Further examples of such unfair side effects of governmental borrowing abound, but I shall not open up this Pandora's box. Suffice it to say that today's taxation of the poor and of the middle class is onerous, so that many of the rich hope to defer tax increases that they alone would pay until all can share in the tax increases or until their unearned income on such deferred amounts exceeds the tax increases their children would pay or until they can find other ways not to pay their fair share. Whether these costs of government are actually shifted unfairly today or are questionably shifted tomorrow so as to be borne primarily by the working middle class is, however, irrelevant to our basic conclusion that the benefits from governmental borrowing do not justify the risks.

Our final test of our proposal to outlaw government debt is to look at those who buy government bonds to see whether they need this investment vehicle that the financial services label the safest investment and, in the process, to consider alternative investments and other means of reducing mandatory government. Who are the lenders who make this trillion-dollar debt possible? They are individuals, rich or poor, citizens or foreigners, governments, local or foreign, and institutions, including business and nonprofit corporations, trusts, and pension plans. The rich have the luxury of a balanced investment portfolio, with many eggs in many baskets, shares of ownership in, or loans to, all the major different types of businesses, so that it is unlikely they would be badly hurt in any recession, and as protection against a great depression, they have tangibles such as gold bullion and objets d'art. The rich do not need government bonds. I believe the poor do not either. Even though they do not have the luxury of a risk-balancing portfolio, alternatives could be made available such as free government insurance covering their bank certificates of deposit up to, say, $50,000, available to those with assets of no more than $100,000, excluding home and automobile; or preferably, they could purchase private insurance in any desired amount.

Domestic local governments have no business being in the investment business, as we have already seen, and so they need no investment vehicles. They should be limited to spending only their tax revenues and to raising through taxes only enough to fund their programs. Even if you want those employed by state and municipal governments to have their pensions funded, there is no need for state or municipal governments to do this themselves. Life insurance companies, for example, for single or periodic payments will relieve them of this risk and at the same time also relieve them of the temptation of invading these funds at times of financial crisis.

If our own citizens and local governments do not need the security of federal bonds, why should they be sold to foreign persons or governments? Do our trade policies require us to do so? Our present substantial trade deficit, another unsightly aspect of current life, baffles me. Personally, I have always had an enormous trade deficit. I have always bought more than I have sold. In fact, I can remember selling very little. This results from my having worked for others all my life. There is nothing wrong with that. They paid me appropriately. If our country's trade deficit becomes as large as mine, relatively speaking, will our people have to work for foreigners not of their choosing? Can our people count on being paid appropriately?

I believe in international free trade. This means that our people may, if they so desire, buy foreign products. Such products often cost less than comparable domestic products, for a variety of possible reasons, such as inferior products or a work force that works harder or longer hours or for less pay than ours. Our people may even buy from foreigners more than they sell to foreigners and thereby create the trade deficit. Then our people will be bartering U.S. dollars for foreign goods, dollars that in foreign hands lose value, because the foreigners cannot use them as effectively as they can their own money. They do not want to buy our products, for a variety of reasons, such as excessive cost or lack of product. Their own producers will not accept U.S. dollars without requiring a premium. So the foreigners decide that the best use of their U.S. dollars is to invest them in our country, in our real estate, in our businesses, and in our government bonds. In wartime such foreign ownership can only exacerbate the conflicts. I conclude, therefore, that substantial trade imbalances are not desirable, at least until we have a world government and its congress provides standards governing international trade and currencies, for example, by amending a written constitution such as is set forth in the appendix. Meanwhile, we should take a balanced view of the foreign investment our trade deficit is causing. On the one hand, we should not act provincially in discouraging both the deficit and foreign investment in view of our desired goal of international free trade. On the other hand, our government should not encourage either and probably should discourage both. My even-handed approach has two aspects.

First, I would outlaw all passive real estate investment for everybody. Earlier in this chapter we concluded that real estate could be owned in stewardship by individuals as necessary for their homes and their own businesses. Hence in order to prohibit passive ownership of real estate all that is required is to exclude from such individual businesses any business that invests in real estate, as contrasted to a business that uses real estate in its operation. For example, you may own and operate an apartment house provided it is managed directly by you or your employee, for whose acts you are responsible. As such you may rent out apartments. You may not, however, be an absentee landlord. Likewise, for example, a mortgage lender upon foreclosure must be prepared to own and operate the business until he can effect a sale. Devices such as leases (except in the case of home rentals) and management contracts will be banned, as they are instruments designed to provide insulation for the owners and thereby enable them to shirk responsibility. The lease has always been a mongrel, part contract, part interest in real estate, mixed property, part personalty, part realty, and was devised at first to evade the laws banning usury. Subject, therefore, to the provisions of our immigration laws, I see no objection to aliens owning homes and businesses in our country. With our abolition of the concept of the corporation and our requirement for responsible operation on site, the likelihood of such ownerships becoming oppressively large would appear to be slight.

One final and completely extraneous thought about real estate is that not all our land need be held in such contemplated residential and private and public business ownership. Taking a cue from the American Indians, our government should set aside vast areas to be without ownership rights in anyone and to be for use by everybody, subject to elaborate restrictions. For example, forest reserves could be set aside for fishing, hunting, camping, hiking, boating, and discreet harvesting of timber, mining of minerals, and reservation of water.

The second aspect of my approach to the trade deficit is to outlaw all governmental borrowing, thereby eliminating investment in U.S. Treasury obligations for everybody. If our people don't need such security, neither do foreigners. Thus to obtain the use of money from foreigners is a transparent gimmick that can only lead to unnecessary trouble. We have seen how our own rich can avoid the tax burden of governmental programs by loaning the government the necessary funds. This was not a pretty picture, but far more frightening to contemplate is the picture of vast amounts of maturing government bonds in the hands of non-tax-paying foreigners at a time of international crisis when the repayment of this debt with interest is competing with the defense requirements of the military for every taxpayer's dollar available in the national budget.

On the other hand, I see no reason for prohibiting foreign investment in our businesses, both equity and debt, on the same terms as are available to our own citizens, as war risks are just another of the many and various risks one assumes in business transactions.

The remaining categories of lenders for whom we are to test the necessity of having the security of government bonds available for their investment are institutions, including business and nonprofit corporations, banks, trusts, and pension plans. Corporations pose no problem, as we have abolished the concept.

Let us double-check our understanding of this. Instead of business corporations we are using sole proprietorships and small partnerships whose members are active in the business. When such businesses require the advantages of bigness, they may either join together in cooperative associations, or, in order to allow people to invest in their ownership, take in inactive but fully liable partners. Their liability can be covered by private insurance. Let me show you how. But first, a diversion into what you need to know about my views of insurance.

My first ideological brush with insurance was years ago, before state law required automobile insurance in minimal amounts. My college roommate mentioned that his father, a clergyman, carried no automobile insurance on their large, old Lincoln. He told his son that his protection came from the Lord. In similar vein, the following short dialogue took place years later at a church forum at which another cleric was trying to increase participation in his church. He asked, "Why do people come to church?"

Someone replied, "For insurance."

"Fire or life?" he shot back.

Implicit in Jesus' first great command to love God is the requirement to follow the will of God and to be responsible and accountable to him. So when the kingdom comes man will not need the expense of insurance, its enormous cost in manpower, the actuaries and all the other nonproductive middlemen involved in deciding and in implementing how much the house must take in in premiums, how much it may pay out in claims, and how much it can retain for the house, in this greatest of all gambling establishments where the winners are the actual losers. When the kingdom comes the members of the voluntary community will see to it responsibly that the homeless are given homes after fires until they once again can carry their own weight, the widows and orphans are provided for after the premature death of the breadwinner until they are able to cope for themselves, and the injured are brought back to health after accidents. Insurance against man-made risks such as theft will become unnecessary, as theft will not exist. But until the kingdom comes, insurance is an entirely reasonable and responsible concept for the voluntary community to use to protect its members against the unfortunate, unexpected happenings in life. Moreover, the insurance middleman is and always has been enormously enterprising in devising ways to provide insurance protection at reasonable cost.

Let me show you how he might structure a way by which I could easily buy coverage for all of the potential liability of the worldwide Exxon corporation at a price commensurate with the value of, say, five or ten shares I might desire to purchase for investment. If Exxon's total insurable potential liability is X trillion dollars and if it has 1 billion shares outstanding, then each share fairly should only bear 100X dollars of such liability. Even though an insurer may insure me in the amount of X trillion dollars, as the total amount any claimant may recover from all shareholders may never exceed the amount of his claim, there is only one risk, for which only one premium should be charged, so by sharing agreements among all the participating insurers, assuming all shareholders covered their risk with insurance, I could receive X trillion dollars of coverage for about the cost of a policy that provides liability protection in a dollar amount equal to 100X times the number of shares I owned. I say "about" as there would need to be an added expense factor to cover this elaborate procedure and documentation. The problem that would occur if some shareholders decided not to buy insurance protection could be avoided by Exxon's selling its shares only to those who bound themselves contractually to buy the required amount of insurance. These contracts would also require that this insurance must be purchased from insurers not affiliated with Exxon.

Voilà. Although abolishing the corporation is not yet an idea whose time has come, it is an entirely reasonable and responsible way to rid ourselves of one of the institutions that exudes irresponsibility today. Note in passing that the law, which has its own conception of responsibility, already has taken preliminary strides in the direction of abolishing the corporation. My first law firm had as clients a group of short-haul truckers. I can remember my shock in learning that it was the common practice of the long-haul trucking industry at that time to carry overweight loads in violation of the weight laws, because the revenue from the excess weight carried exceeded the amount of the fine even if the trucker were apprehended. Jail was no deterrent because the trucking corporation was the criminal. How do you jail an artificial person? Today, particularly in cases involving hazardous waste and pollution, the legislature and the courts are piercing the corporate veil and sending offending corporate officers and directors to jail. In civil cases of every nature the prospect of directors and officers and even principal stockholders being found individually liable for corporate wrongdoing has greatly increased.

The nonprofit corporation poses entirely different problems from the business corporation. What responsibility should charities and their owners and employees have for their activities? In common law both king and charity were not liable for negligence, though for different reasons. In my practice I found the law of nonprofit corporations most frustrating with which to work because the few cases there were did not clarify or resolve the issues. Could it be that this body of law had never been developed in the crucible of carefully written court and legal texts because, as lawyers do not dare to bill charities much, they do not care to spend much time in this type of practice? My recollection is that in Pennsylvania in my lifetime nonprofit hospitals have become liable for their negligence because the court did not want to discriminate against those hospitals that for one reason or another carried liability insurance. When it comes to charity we have another encounter between the law and the spirit. I do not want the state to favor charity, for example, with tax exemptions, but I do not want the law to require an admission fee in the form of insurance premiums before one may do acts of charity. Just as the Good Samaritan statutes enacted in recent years have made it possible for a doctor to render emergency treatment at the scene of an accident in a state in which he is not licensed to practice without becoming liable for negligence for thus acting, so by extension I suggest that bona fide charities and their owners and employees should be exempt from all liability for negligence arising in the performance of their charitable activity. We do not want malpractice lawsuits like that of heirs of a competent, uninfluenced, wealthy spinster suing a priest on allegations she had bequeathed all she had to the poor while acting upon his unlicensed homilectic advice.

The definition of what constitutes a bona fide charity will be troublesome. It will be considerably less broad than that of nonprofit corporations in today's Internal Revenue Code. The definition should include:

1. A limit on the amount of salary the charity's members or employees may receive, which must be well below salaries for comparable work in the business community. Most doctors, for example, will not qualify. You will remember we proposed doing away with medical malpractice suits and let the medical associations be responsible for the quality of medical care.
2. A restriction on the type of activity that qualifies to include churches, schools, hospitals, food providers, and shelters, but not artistic, political, or scientific organizations.
3. A limitation on the scope of the exempt activity. For example, all charities must carry automobile insurance like everyone else, but the exempt charities will not be liable for malpractice.

Under what form of legal entity these bona fide charities operate would not appear to be material. Other nonprofit corporations should be treated like business entities, that is, like sole proprietorships and partnerships.

Finally, just as we determined that both rich and poor people do not need to be able to protect their savings by investments in government bonds, so for the same reasons charities do not need this protection for their endowments, whether large or small.

We consider next the need banks may have for governmental obligations as an investment vehicle. If it were not for banks, all commerce would have to be done in bartering transactions or through the use of personal credit, and the latter would restrict commerce to that between trusting parties. Banks are, therefore, necessary to make available the means of exchange in all commercial transactions, and for this service they are entitled to be paid. They are also necessary as depositories of funds needed by investors for liquidity, and for this safekeeping they are also entitled to compensation. The minute banks pay their depositors interest on their deposits rather than charge them a safekeeping fee they become financial middlemen dealing with other people's money. Contrary to all I have written about the securities markets, I believe regulation of the banking business by the federal government is necessary at this time. A sound banking system is the heart of the economy of this country. Only it enables goods to pass daily from producer through distributor to consumer and all other private and public business to be transacted, both commercial and financial, and with few exceptions, only it protects the funds all people need for a rainy day.

I envision various thrusts to such regulation. Banking should be restricted to short-term operations. I see no objection if the banks wish to acquire funds by paying interest to their depositors and lend such funds for emergency or other short-term needs to personal and business borrowers who pay an interest cost in excess of that the bank pays its depositors in order to cover the bank's expense, its profit, and a reserve factor for bad loans. In a period of highly fluctuating interest rates, the bank can easily adjust its interest rates on short-term deposits and short-term loans and maintain its solvency, thereby enabling it to carry on its primary businesses of exchange and safekeeping of depositors' funds. Long-term lending jeopardizes such liquidity, as do long-term interest commitments on deposits. Moreover, the minimal differentials in the interest rates paid to the depositors for tying up their money for greater periods of time do not justify their loss of liquidity, flexibility, and incentive in embarking on a meaningful investment program of their own. Accordingly, the banks' unseemly huckstering of such minutia should be outlawed. This same treatment should be given to the banks' unseemly huckstering of their funds for use as loans. Rate competition between banks is to be encouraged, but excessive borrowing by the people is not desirable.

The bank's reserves should be kept separate from its other funds and preferably, in part at least, in a central reserve bank. The government might give the banks for maintaining these reserves some quid pro quo arising out of the money-making powers of the government, which we have already discussed. This is an exception that proves the following rule: namely, in transforming any activity on our way to the kingdom from one that is provided for by mandatory government to one that is taken care of by a voluntary community the transition should be clean-cut. Let us not hear of cooperation between the private and the public sectors. Just as one does not mix apples and oranges, so the mandatory community by its nature cannot cooperate. It can only mandate. Any attempt to make believe there is such cooperation can only be ineffectual and a waste of taxpayers' money. The standards that govern these two communities are absolutely different.

Probably the most restrictive aspect of the regulation I would propose for commercial banks is that their principal owners be prohibited from entering other businesses, particularly from entering investment banking. Last week I read that the chairman of the Federal Reserve Board and several influential senators were suggesting that commercial banks be allowed to enter into investment banking so that all bankers would be free to play on the same level field. They suggested, further, that the depositors of the commercial bank could be protected from losses in the bank's investment operations by having the bank create a holding company to be the parent of two separate corporate subsidiaries, one for the commercial bank and the other for investment operation. Even if such corporate protection were eliminated, the same technical result could be achieved by legislatively prohibiting creditors of the owners or of the investment banking operation from reaching the funds of the commercial bank. Either way, however, I believe the concept is misguided. In this competitive field today merely the suspicion of trouble in the investment banking operation would adversely affect the amount of deposits held by the commercial bank. So the owners can be expected voluntarily to do all they possibly can to bolster up the investment operation, even at the risk of hurting the commercial bank. For example, it is so easy to take an aggressive position in the financial statements that assets could be freed up and bank reserves easily siphoned over to help the investment operation when it was in trouble. For this reason I think commercial banking should be kept out of the risk-taking activities of investment bankers.

If this regulation strikes you as excessive and out-of-character in this book, then I recommend that the activities of the commercial bank and its owners be limited to the exchange and safekeeping functions for a fee and that the bank and its owners be kept entirely out of the investing business of borrowing and lending. A safe, sound, stable, even stodgy, national banking system is of paramount importance to the national economy. In conclusion, banks have no need to invest in the security of government bonds and their owners, like the owners of corporations and trusts, are comparable to both rich and poor people in not needing the availability of government bonds.

This leaves us with only pensions for consideration. Pensions are the litmus paper by which one can tell whether he is a spirit-centered or a law-centered person and whether he is more comfortable in a spirit-oriented or a law-oriented society. There are mainly two types of pensions: public and private. The public pension is called Social Security and is funded primarily by tax-deductible contributions of the employer and by non-tax-deductible contributions of the employee, both mandatory until retirement. The system has never been actuarially sound since its inception. Hence the mandated contributions are ever increasing in amount, so that one may fairly say younger workers are contributing to the pensions of older workers. The private pension is primarily the qualified pension plan under which the employer obtains an immediate tax deduction for amounts he commits himself to paying, and customarily then funds, to provide pension payments to retired workers, so that such funds have the benefit of a tax-free inside interest buildup, as the worker is not taxed until receipt of retirement payments.

There are two ways to look at pensions. One way is this: As laborers we are entitled to our hire, but in both types of pensions we as laborers are being deprived of a substantial part of our hire when we earn it. We are being treated as children who are being cared for by government and by employer, both of whom know what is best for us. Our spirit is stifled because for most of us outrageous living expense uses up all the milk our wages produce and the cream, the amount we could save, invest, and use to develop self-reliance and self-respect, is skimmed off and given to others to use. Think of the millions of middlemen in the pension system who suck off these earnings of the wage earners, bureaucrats in practically every community, technical experts and clerks in practically every business, the number of which, as in Aesop's fable, daily increases geometrically in the sad attempt of the law to make fair something that can never be made fair because it represents a denial of man's spirit. I would hope some reader would challenge me thus: "What are you bitching about? Your pensions give you the freedom to write your book." My reply: "My joy in life was walking up mountains, a joy that arthritic legs now proscribe. Lifelong dreams of the tops of mountains outside the forty-eight states, dreams of Alaska, South America, and especially Switzerland and Nepal, will forever remain just dreams. The system withheld from me the cream of my work when I needed it most by finding me unworthy of the fullness of my hire. I know I would not have spent the cream foolishly. Whether I could have saved it prudently and sufficiently I will never know. I was deprived of the opportunity to have tried, and thus deprived, I remain unfulfilled and bitter."

Contrast this way of looking at pensions with this next way: A function of government is to meet the physical needs of its people if the family and voluntary community fail to do so. In the case of the elderly, this involves subsidizing living expenses and especially health expense when they are no longer able to work or to find work and have used up their savings. Government, the master planner, the great white father, guides its children through the Strait of Messina with these thoughts: Many workers cannot refrain from spending all they earn and, indeed, in addition, all they can get their hands on through borrowing. They are glad to shirk the responsibility of saving for their own retirement and to let Uncle Sam do it for them. For these reasons, government sets up its own mandatory program and gives tax incentives to business to set up their voluntary programs, to withhold from the breadwinners amounts to fund pensions for their retirement. By these means government protects itself to some extent against having to care for the idle elderly. What more logical way can there by for handling this problem? In an attempt to help you determine your own position let me set forth some considerations.

1. I doubt that making pensions optional is a feasible alternative. With respect to the Social Security System, as it is not actuarially sound, there is no practical way to give uncovered workers equal benefits. I believe this is one reason why the system has always covered all workers and not just the lower-income workers who provide the rationale for this awfully wasteful program. With respect to business pensions, one of their main attractions to the employer is that, despite all the Aesop-fabled regulations regarding portability and vesting, pragmatically speaking, business pensions tend to enslave many employees. Pensions tend to get the worker to work now and be paid later. He has to continue to work, just as did the workers in a bygone age who lived in the company town. They could not quit, because their debt to the company store for food and clothing exceeded the amount in their paychecks.

Moreover, I doubt that it would be practical for an employer to make participation in the company's pension plan optional, as it would certainly appear to be unfair for tax reasons. If the employee who opted to receive the equivalent in cash of the amount that the employer would otherwise fund into the retirement plan on his behalf were required by government to pay immediate income tax thereon he would unfairly lose the benefit of the tax-free interest buildup. If, unfairly to other taxpayers, he were not required to pay such tax immediately, there would probably be few who would choose to be covered by the plan.

2. Personally I feel if Social Security were abolished, the cost to government of unemployment compensation for healthy elderly poor unable to find jobs would be less than the cost to government of the Social Security system today. I make this statement realizing that mandatory contributions of employer and employee shield the government from direct costs for Social Security. I am talking about the indirect costs such as the loss of tax revenues arising from the presently tax-deductible employer contributions. I am also talking about healthy elderly. Elderly who are too unhealthy to hold any job probably pose a Medicare problem rather than a Social Security one.
3. On the other hand, if my feeling is incorrect, if most workers would spend the increased amounts they would receive and not save for their retirement and if they would look to the substitute unemployment compensation to meet expenses of retirement, then until such time as they become self-reliant I can see a desirability in retaining Social Security and business pensions, because the voluntary community presently is unable to assume this burden. Hence although the next

exit (#8) is for those whose view of society is centered in the law, I can understand disagreement on pensions coming from even those who are spirit-centered.

Does this equivocal treatment of pensions offend you? Does it bother you that I offer no blueprint and no timetable to plot a systematic transition from the law-centered mandatory community to a spirit-centered voluntary community? All I offer is a hodgepodge of situations, some in which compulsion is increased over what we presently have, some in which compulsion is decreased, and some in which I leave it up for grabs, all depending upon the way I feel under the exigencies of the moment. But I submit you should be neither offended nor bothered by this. Jesus tells us the kingdom will come like a thief in the night and our task is to be prepared for its coming. So I am not overly concerned where you come out on any of these particular situations I discuss, provided you approach each such situation holding the beliefs and standards we have developed and then attempt reasonably to apply these standards to the situation of the moment. This is in no way comparable to what has been called situation ethics, where what is right varies depending upon the facts of the particular situation in which one finds himself. We prepare for the coming of the kingdom by trying to do what is right except only when our God-given minds logically lead us to conclude that it is absolutely necessary to do what is wrong, and then in doing the wrong we ask God to forgive us. I believe once everyone takes this uniform approach to all problems the reasonable differences of opinion will become manageable and, willy-nilly, a distant view of the kingdom will appear to all.

Before leaving the subject of pensions, I should add that I wholeheartedly favor the purchase of private retirement annuities by any inclined individual with the use of his own after-tax savings. Insofar as public and business pensions are concerned, however, they both suppress the spirit and are flawed in their thus trying to do good through coercion. Finally, funds required for pensions have no need to be invested in government bonds. If we discard the pension system, there would be no such funds. If we keep Social Security, the government automatically acquires these funds. If we keep business pensions, businesses can use for their pension funds the same investment programs their owners use for their own funds, but with restrictions against investment in the business of the owner.

Having decided that the government does not need to borrow and none of the public needs the security of government bonds for investment, once we pay off the present public debt, we will have solved the problem of the budget deficit. There is no way there can be a deficit if it is unlawful for the government to borrow or use its credit, because the government will then be able to spend only what it raises from taxes and seigniorage. Incidentally, this neat handling of the budget deficit has deprived our farmer of what the experts consider to be the safest investment vehicle in which to put his rainy-day savings. Fortunately, we have seen in the process that deposits in soundly regulated banks are an alternative. We have also seen that by eliminating governmental borrowing we have saved him his share of the substantial taxes required to pay interest on the public debt. Earlier we saw that by deregulating the securities markets we likewise saved him his share of the substantial costs of this unnecessary regulation. Such savings have all come from direct reduction of governmental activity.

We now tackle the problem from a different perspective and look at an indirect way for our farmer to save. In the process we hope to find other appropriate vehicles for his increased savings. To accomplish these objectives we shall look at some occupations that may unnecessarily add their charges to the farmer's marketing costs or that may not pay their fair share of taxes, thereby indirectly making him carry their burden. The starting point is this: when one comes between two people in such a way that an onlooker may question the desirability of the intervention, the intervenor may be called a middleman. Upon such questioning, the middleman may be found to be desirable or not. We here begin this line of questioning.

Media comes from the Latin word *medius* and means "middle." Hence the media is the type species of the genus middlemen. These middlemen are those who work with newspapers, magazines, radio, television, and other communications. Were I to tackle the problems of the media, here are positions I would expect to take:

There will always be a need for reporters, for they bring to our attention facts of current events as they happen before the teachers are able to assemble the available facts, digest them, and teach us from them.

Articles or programs containing opinions, and expressly so identified, are not objectionable provided everyone has reasonable access to this marketplace of ideas, but reporters should stick to the facts without unbalanced presentation, opinion, gossip, rumor, or innuendo.

Just as there should be separation of church and state, so should there be separation of media and state. Government should ensure the media's freedom without establishing or supporting the media.

I pass over any detailed discussion of standards appropriate for the media, because the media are obviously desirable up to a point and because the media as such do not push me around. Not that the media do not irritate me every bit as much as do churchmen and politicians, but I can avoid direct contact with the media in a way I cannot avoid religion because of my conscience or government because of its compulsions.

My reservations about the media, especially about national television, arise mainly from a fear that an open marketplace may not be at work here. I fear I might find an unholy, though unpremeditated, alliance between big business, big media, and big government, glued together by the crassest of the middlemen, the advertisers. This alliance I envision enables its participants to live off the people by glutting them with bread and circuses much in the same way that the Roman emperors kept the public occupied in a far less complicated age. My first partial insight into this alliance came at the age of ten. For each *Saturday Evening Post* I sold for its stated price of a nickel I was paid a nickel. Confused, I was told circulation had to be maintained during the summer to be able to collect the advertising revenues that paid the twenty cents it cost the publisher to put out each magazine. I was still confused. The practice smelt. The stench remains unto this day. I kept the hard-earned nickels. My boss would not have cared if I had thrown the magazines away. This insight explains why I must stomach the demeaning advertising junk in order to see, hear, or read the daily news and why the public must be tempted with free time-wasting spectator sports and soap operas in order for television stations to maintain their viewers and, hence, their advertising revenues. If this is the way the open, self-supporting marketplace works, then it is up to me to try to *e*ducate the people to want a better diet than bread, spectator sports, and commercials, in fair competition with those who try to *in*duce the people to use their products. This is the age-old problem of trying to lead *out* of the darkness into the light and not back into the darkness.

Unfortunately, this marketplace is not self-supporting. My ten-year-old partial insight contemplated an alliance of only big business and big media. I did not comprehend big government's involvement until after my legal education. That is why I recommend to any young reader of this book who is interested in its subject matter that he graduate from law school after college without worrying about what use he plans to make of this training. For it is this background that enables me clearly to see that I am to blame for the foul activity in this marketplace. How? Because I pay for it. Advertising expenses are tax-deductible. To the extent business does not pay its share of taxes I pay a greater share. To keep advertisers and their revenues the media must guarantee viewers. The nickel that the media paid me sixty years ago has been inflated into the multimillions that television pays others to attract viewers in the never-ending upward spiraling of advertising costs, business tax deductions, and increases in my tax payments. The solution cries out for implementation. Eliminate advertising expense as a tax deduction for business and at the same time prohibit business from adding it to the cost of their product. To eliminate this tax deduction we do not even have to change the law. All that is required is that the revenue service and the courts interpret it properly. The code provides that in arriving at net taxable income there may be deducted from gross income received upon the sale of products all the costs of raw materials and of the manufacturing process as well as other ordinary and *necessary* business expense. Our advertising orgy, this nonsense, is not necessary. To prohibit business from passing on unreasonable advertising costs to the consumer may require mandated labeling disclosures. Then let business advertise all they want to. Our farmer, the public, and I will no longer have to subsidize this ugly practice. If big business and big media have to do the paying, you will shortly see it shrivel.

Who am I to presume to state that advertising is not a necessary tax-deductible expense? To answer this question I must first be sure you are acquainted with what I believe to be one of the finest concepts the law has given man, a concept that avoids wrangling. It is called, the burden of proof, and it means that the one who has this burden must prove his point to the satisfaction of the one who interprets and applies the standards, regardless of whether his opponent makes a good counteravailing argument or not. Now the purpose of this book is to give a vision of the kingdom and to show the straight and narrow path to get to it. The way is to test every activity against the standard of righteousness and to allow each person voluntarily to follow the right as he sees the right. This way precludes compelling anyone from doing anything unless absolutely necessary. Therefore, it is he who uses compulsion who has the burden every time of proving its necessity. It is up to me on my attempt up this highway to put the point in issue, which I have done, but I do not have to prove that the costs of advertising are unnecessary. I do not even have to have an alternative way for producers to publicize their products, for the media to fund their activity, or for the government to keep the people informed. We who seek the kingdom must raise the issues, even though the subject matter may be complex, intimidating, and unfamiliar, so that those who do things saying their compulsions are necessary are put to their proof.

Quite frankly, I have seen no proof in this case. Advertisers, instead of trying to turn the public to their product casually, the meaning of the word *advert*, have become pervertisers trying to turn the public intensely, the meaning of the word *pervert*. Turn all the way round, boy. Television companies, in order to fill their houses to collect the big advertising revenues, have tried to glamorize their product by such methods as paying annual salaries of over a million dollars each to employees who merely tell you what happened in the news yesterday from reports furnished them and by such methods as paying sports teams millions for television rights so they in turn can pay their players millions. Meanwhile the government forces the individual taxpayers to subsidize this entertainment they are being given without freedom of choice.

Why don't thinking people complain? The abuse could be easily remedied by the government's disallowing as business tax deductions such unreasonably high salaries and unreasonably high advertising expenses. Let me list some reasons, some excuses, people give for not complaining:

Innocence. I don't want to get involved. That's a messy business.

Ignorance. I feel the only way I pay for my sports programs on television is by looking at the commercials.

Indifference to the rights of others. I like the national sports games. I have a good deal. I get for nothing at home what it would cost me hundred of dollars to go to the arenas to see.

Interference with another's business. If I go against advertisers' deductions they may go after mine. Let me develop the full thrust of this excuse. Today's intertwining of voluntary and mandatory communities sometimes makes it difficult to find the way to the kingdom. The church should protect the flock, and if the flock is being financially oppressed it should speak out. "What!" you exclaim. "And bring into question the tax exemptions and charitable tax deductions from which the church benefits?" To this I reply, "Man needs God and not vice versa." I am unable to believe the continued propagation of the Gospel lies in the hands of Caesar or the continued dissemination of the news lies in tax exemptions and deductions that Caesar provides. What I am able to believe is this: with respect to the welfare of the church, just as abolishing the tax deductibility of advertising expense would result indirectly in tax savings for the general public, so abolishing the tax exemptions given charitable and nonprofit institutions and the tax deductions given donors for contributions to these institutions would result in tax savings for the public, including church members. Such savings would enable church members voluntarily to contribute amounts in excess of what the churches would lose from the repeal of their tax exemptions and from the drop in contributions resulting from the repeal of the charitable deduction. The secular games people play with the tax laws to transfer the costs of their pet projects to the public cut the umbilical cord of responsibility flowing between man's spirit and his actions. If you want to have your eyebrows raised just rub your nose in what many of these so-called charities spend their billions on. Birthrights sold for a mess of porridge always produce such progeny. Similarily, I believe the dissemination of the news is not dependent upon tax deductions for advertising expense. There will always be those who idealistically view the publishing of the news and editorializing upon it as their missionary calling, without needing the motivation of fabulous monetary rewards to fulfill this natural desire to gossip, and there will always be those willing to pay the modest amounts required to be kept informed. Finally, we have already seen how businesses can properly bear the costs of advertising their products. Now I ask: have the necessitarians met their burden of proof to support their unjustly placing these additional tax loads upon you? Neither innocence, ignorance, nor even wise and prudent excuses should prevent you from making those who would impose tax increases upon you, directly or deviously, explain, and convince you of, their need. The ninth exit on the highway to the kingdom is for those who have excuses for not moving ahead. And so we leave our first middlemen, the media, representing the species most typical of the genus, and the advertisers where we found them and conclude they are desirable up to a point.

The middlemen that our farmer and other producers probably first encounter are distributors of their products to the consumer. Admittedly desirable are these transporters, merchants, storekeepers, and their helpers. Also desirable in any society are the caretaker services, the services that take care of society. Although these professionals are not middlemen, I list them here lest you fear I have overlooked their importance, namely, the doctors, lawyers, ministers, teachers, economists, accountants, all types of government workers including the military, and, provided they are not offended by their inclusion, the scientists and artists, as well as the staff in each group.

Now at length we come to the middlemen whose desirability we wish to question, the middlemen involved in the financial markets. You have already noted my eagerness to forgo the costly regulation of these markets, except for commercial banking. Looking at the numbers of middlemen engaged in these markets, do we find them all desirable? How many different types do we need, for example, for an investor such as our farmer to be able to make a loan to, or buy a share of, a business? Well, if it is a custom-made transaction, the investor and the business would each need a lawyer, an accountant, and a banker or financial consultant. If it is a ready-made transaction such as a purchase or sale on the financial exchanges of an interest in a publicly held company, then the investor and the seller may need, besides the exchange personnel, either a broker, a financial consultant, or a bank. I say "may" because my father-in-law, a bank vice president, was so contemptuous of the way investment brokers churned accounts for commissions that when, shortly after I married his daughter, he saw I was determined to put some money into blue chip stocks he insisted I pay a bank of my choice a couple of additional dollars to make the purchase for me in order to keep brokers away from me and vice versa; he knew I could not afford a financial consultant.

In addition to the above financial middlemen, there are hosts of others:

1. The traders, those who make their living by buying low and selling high as soon as possible. These speculators come in as many different varieties as the Compositae and are as difficult to name and identify. Often they deal with other people's money. They present the form of gambling we have already decried.

2. The investment companies who sell their stock to the public and with the proceeds from such sales buy shares or obligations of operating businesses or governmental obligations so that their investors may benefit from a diversified portfolio. These investment companies also come in countless varieties.
3. The trust companies, whose business is to take the investors' funds and manage them under varying degrees of instruction or supervision.
4. Finally, there are the salesmen who make their living selling all these different financial offerings to the public.

It strikes me that, except for trust companies who enable an investor's investments pass to the next generation, an individual investor, such as a well-to-do farmer, needs no more middlemen than those required for the custom-made transaction when he invests in a local business whose principals and operations he knows and respects and those required for the ready-made transaction when he invests in a blue chip company with a fine, longstanding national reputation. Such investments would also provide our country with a good mix of local and national businesses. If the investor wishes help in deciding upon his blue chip investments, especially if he is considering investing in a comparatively new company, I see no objection in his paying a reputable financial consultant a fee for his counsel. Nothing that has been said should prevent the investor from investing heavily in his own operating business, if he has one, provided he keeps a diversified portfolio for a rainy day.

How does one arrive at a proper fee for such a financial consultant? How does one decide how much any laborer should be paid? I suppose the starting point is that, as between parties having equal bargaining power, the laborer should charge what the traffic will bear. The farmer, as a sole proprietor, does not get paid for his labor. He gets paid for his products what the traffic will bear, hopefully in an open marketplace. If he works long hours or under adverse conditions, theoretically, at least, this is under this control. His employees and those of other producers, however, present a different problem. For example, a pieceworker, an elderly lady employed in a cannery who is paid by the number of sardines she can behead and betail and place in cans in a day, is paid in an entirely different way for what she produces. Her nimble fingers are a wonder to behold, but their bandages belie the fairness of the practice. If a trade union organizes the plant to give her equal bargaining power there is always the danger, which we have alluded to before, of those defending the oppressed going over the murky line and, like a seesaw, upsetting the balance in bargaining power in the other direction so that the former oppressors become the new oppressed. Note we have just picked up another group of middlemen, those who live off dues paid by the downtrodden to those who will lead them to higher ground. I believe mandatory government should keep out of this balancing act except to prevent violence and fraud. Specifically, there is no need for workers to receive tax deductions for union dues, just as there is no need for do-gooders to receive tax deductions for charitable gifts, and both deductions should be eliminated. If the union does increase the old lady's bargaining power, I would hope she could use it to get a higher and satisfactory hourly wage, so that she could have the satisfaction of knowing she was being paid for what she did and not for the time she puts in.

Comparable to bad union leaders are the high-living television evangelists, an unsightly phenomenon, which I believe will disappear with the abolition of tax deductions for advertising and of all tax benefits for charity, so that you and I do not have to join in paying for these abusers. The voluntary community should teach people that excessive compensation for doing good for others is a danger signal. Good works are freely done. Indeed, the tenth exit is for those who want personally to profit financially from staying on the highway to the kingdom.

So much for the problem of how to fix wages for those who work in production and in distribution. The next question is: should those who work in service activities also charge what the traffic will bear? Here we confront the problem of equal bargaining power from a different perspective. In the marketplace of labor in commerce the imbalancing factor is usually the poverty of the worker. Both employer and employee have a fair idea of what a decent wage should be. They can look at what workers are getting in other plants and in comparable businesses. In the marketplace of labor in service activities the imbalancing factor is the absence of immediately available comparisons. Lawyers often have minimum fee schedules, which are more often ignored than observed, because each case is different. The lawyers' code of ethics requires a fee commensurate with the difficulty of the undertaking, the time spent, the prior knowledge and experience brought to the task, and the amount of other work lost by taking the representation. For example, your lawyer should not represent your competition. Thank God I was a salaried house counsel; otherwise I would have starved from wasting time fixing fees. Again, however, I conclude there can be no standard for determining the charge for labor in the service industries other than what the traffic will bear in an open marketplace, mandatory government should remain aloof, and the voluntary community should attempt to find pro bono laborers for poor people needing such services. So if our investor wishes to have the aid of a financial consultant in choosing his investments I suggest he ask his broker or business friends for suggestions and pick one of proven reliability within his price range.

The exercise we have just gone through in these last pages was a necessary prelude to this, my fugue on the salesman. To have a good insurance and financial salesman whom you trust, with whom you work well, and who is knowledgeable is one of life's minor joys. A bad salesman, however, is worse than the advertiser. The advertiser as pervertiser merely turns you intensely toward his product; the bad salesman gives you the shaft itself. In his fraternity the term for this is *the close.* To help one be able to tell the difference between a good and a bad salesman, it may be enough for some merely to recognize the difference between the salesman and the consultant. This would not be enough for me. I would prefer the consultant. I would pay him a fixed fee. He would give me advice based on his expert knowledge. Then I would make the decision. This differs from the salesman. His fee, in the form of a commission, a percentage of what he sells, is paid by the seller with whom he holds a contract, yet the buyer relies on the salesman for advice as to the best product to buy and the best cost to pay. The code of the salesman is to give the client the advice the salesman himself would follow; the code of the counselor is to give the client the benefit of the counselor's knowledge so that the client can make his own decision more intelligently. The temptation for the person who buys from a salesman is to shirk responsibility for the decision by believing he is receiving good advice gratuitously when in fact the buyer does not even know how much the salesman makes on the sale. For example, customarily the life insurance salesman receives up front over 50 percent of the first year's premium, with more deferred. The temptation of the salesman is to let his need for the sale distort his advice and to let his desire to control money ignore the client's learning process. I call this the Daddy knows best approach. If you can find a financial salesman whose integrity, intelligence, and knowledge enable him to rise above these conflicts you are indeed fortunate. Again, I see no reason for government to be involved in the relationship between the salesman and his client until fraud appears. Governmental attempts to put mandatory limits on the amount of commissions have been of doubtful value. Disallowing business tax deductions for excessive selling commissions and taking away investors' tax deductions for excessive fees paid counselors would be more satisfactorily inhibiting.

You will note I have confused the different functions of insurance salesman and insurance consultant on the one hand and on the other those of financial salesman and financial consultant. As I am more acquainted with the former, I used them as my model. Actually, insurance consultants are not as common as financial consultants, but often one person wears more than one hat, sometimes all four hats. The important point is that in insurance the adviser is not tempted by much money, only premiums and commissions, but in the financial markets the salesman may control the investor's life savings. It is this desire of the swarms of financial salesmen to control money that provides the base for the pyramid of financial middlemen.

We are now in a position to tackle the problem of getting rid of the unproductive middlemen in the financial markets, the barracudas whom we have earlier described and whom we are treating and tolerating like unregulated gamblers under the common law. Remember, we do not make them outlaws. What we do is remove any support we give these people, like support through the taxes we pay or in the funds we make available to them. If we cut off their funds they are out of business, for they live on other people's money. First, let us see how the financial markets work. Here I overstate for clarity, like a cartoonist. Once the swarms of financial salesmen get control of the investor's money, the financial institutions for whom these salesmen work—whether brokerage houses, trust departments of banks, mutual funds, investment trusts, investment companies, or partnerships—must invest the investor's monies, either as principal or as agent, ultimately in productive businesses, although often through many intermediary holding companies or other financial institutions. Such investing places a great responsibility on the investment managers, who according to current wisdom have all reached in their own organizations the level of their incompetence. These managers, therefore, seek to avoid responsibility for their actions by hiring and relying upon hordes of experts, often called consultants. This practice is known as the CYA (Cover Your Ass) technique. The conflicts of interest all these people have are awesome. Brokers buy and sell for their own account and for your account, often the same stock the same day, at different prices. Consulting firms advise businesses when to take certain actions, such as declaring dividends, going into the marketplace for capital or loans, selling a subsidiary, going into a new venture, or merging with or acquiring another company. Underwriters in these consulting firms are often at work on such deals the same day investment advisers in these same firms are recommending to their clients and to the firm itself what stocks to buy and sell. As the short-term bottom line controls all decision making, no wonder the gutsiest risk taker, especially one who knows what is going on, makes it to the top of the heap.

Now one way you do not remove support for bad people is to outlaw activity that is intrinsically good. All such laws accomplish is to give the bad lawbreakers an unfair advantage over the law-abiding public. So any attempt to prohibit trading on insider information, any attempt to require these financial houses, for example, to Berlin-Wall off their various divisions in order to prevent their salesmen from receiving hot tips from their underwriters, is bound to support the gutsiest of the risk takers and to fail in its purpose. In other words, I believe all of us should bring all the knowledge we possibly can to bear upon every problem we tackle in life. Specifically, we should invest when we have insiders' information. To invest without such information is irresponsible with few exceptions such as investments in blue chip stocks for the long pull in national companies with fine track records and with reputable management known for not taking undue personal advantage of their corporate opportunities. That is why I like to see one invest in local businesses, the operations, operators, and owners of which he is intimately acquainted with. Let the big boys in the financial institutions using only the institutions' own money and let individual gamblers using only their own money be the ones who risk putting their money into the hands of the big-time speculators. Let the ordinary person know he is gambling when he gives his money to any financial institution in return for only a share of its stock, and let him know he is not being responsible for the use of his money. If this advice were followed and if pensions were abolished, the financial sharks would self-destruct for dearth of OPM (Other People's Money; remember Fifi!).

One way government can remove support for these barracudas is to see to it that they pay their taxes. In yesterday's newspaper, the financial reporter wrote that short-selling was increasing the Dow's fluctuations. The Dow is now at all-time record highs. The article pointed out that as investors wanted to cash out to reap their huge profits and at the same time retain an option to regain their positions after the precipitious drop came, they were borrowing stock (not money) from brokers for a fee and agreeing to return the borrowed stock in a few months. Then they immediately sold the borrowed stock to reap the huge profit, fully expecting to be able to buy the same number of shares back later at a much lower price on the open market in order to be able to give the stock back to the broker in repayment of the loan in time. The article concluded that as the expected fall has not yet taken place, these short sellers are now adding fuel to the market's rise by having to meet their loan repayments by buying stock at the higher prices, to their great loss. I will bet that this problem is caused by government. Why did the investor not just sell his own stock in the first place and buy his position back later only if the price had dropped as expected? This is what he was trying to do, in fact. The answer probably is that such a sale and repurchase would have produced for him a prohibitive taxable gain, which he avoids by pretending to borrow. A tax law properly enforced could eliminate such nonsense.

We have now concluded our questioning of the desirability of the many middlemen that come between our farmer, who is playing for us the part of the producer in our society, and those that consume his produce. We have seen that many of these middlemen constitute an unnecessary financial burden for him. Before that, in our search for a profitable yet safe place for him to invest his rainy-day savings, we have seen how all sorts of unnecessary governmental burdens whittle away at these savings: unfair taxes, useless regulation, costs of avoidable public debt, and worthless services. In the process we have witnessed some ugly sights in our society. Can you imagine a heavier burden or uglier sights? Well, consider for a moment the three-quarters of the world's population who are living in poverty in the countries of the so-called third world. I believe these countries include all of Asia, Africa, and Central and South America, with a few exceptions, such as Japan. How can the workers of the rest of the world possibly feed such numbers? The mere thought is enough to drive any Christian from God's at-hand kingdom for this world right into the consoling embrace of everlasting life, just as in similar fashion the solitary prospector who roamed the lonely vast expanse of our western wilderness over a century ago, when disabled, would down the vial of laudanum carefully kept for the occasion moments before the surrounding howling wolf pack came in for the kill. Yes, I believe the feeding of the world in the future will place the heaviest burden upon our farmer. The problem is already upon us in the form of a trillion-dollar third-world debt, a little of which we are already forgiving.

By now you know I do not care much for loans. If the loan is to be made because the recipient is worthy, I prefer to take the transaction out of the money-making category of investment and view it as a gift. Gifts have the potential for spiritual ripples of infinite duration. Loans, however, such as government-subsidized loans to students, have the potential for the borrower's going into bankruptcy before ever even going into business. Nor would I saddle developing third-world countries with debt in an attempt to help them. I disagree that this helps them become fiscally responsible. Lending banks and lending governments regularly compound international problems in such a blatant attempt thus to eat their cake and have it, too. What an ugly sight!

Now where does this leave us in our search for the kingdom? In our meanderings have we, like Whiffenpoofs, lost our way and gone astray singing our "baas" in some Phrygian hall? We started this chapter thinking of man's physical needs and how to fulfill them with as little governmental involvement as possible. We have seen how we might obtain water and food, but our last paragraph would leave many of the peoples of the world starving. Where's the integrity of my message? Men of goodwill often find their integrity in giving of themselves to their needy neighbors, no matter where they find the need, whether next door or on the other side of the world. They react to needs without a thought of priorities and consequences. If tens of thousands of Sudanese are starving to death today, they send food, hoping it reaches the starving survivors. They have no time nor stomach for other considerations. To a great extent the missionary activity of the church follows this pattern. I am trying to do more by suggesting a framework for action, but as of now I have no solution for third-world problems and reluctantly leave these problems to this commendable missionary activity of others.

The framework I am suggesting is that with respect to communities that have no viable government a government be created forthwith. My example was a constitution for the beginning of a world government. With respect to communities that have viable governments, conscious attempts should daily be made to turn over mandatory functions to voluntary communities, preferably the church. The reason is that only voluntary communities can do what is right and good. This statement is almost a truism. The voluntary community can only do what everybody either agrees is right or lets pass as right. Otherwise dissenters walk away and you no longer have a voluntary community. Mandatory communities cannot do what is right because it is never right to force another to do your will. Governments can only do what is necessary. Sometimes it is necessary to take forcibly from one and give to another. Such compulsion is present in every function of government. I have little trouble in understanding what is right, but I vacillate in deciding what is necessary. I know that what I believe to be necessary another may believe to be wrong. Certainly government should try, therefore, to do the least necessary. But what does this mean? Machiavelli suggests that it means what the times require, but who is to know what that means? Is it ever necessary to lie? Remember the *Pueblo*. The admiral told us that the ship was not within Vietnam's territorial waters and that he told the Vietcong that it was in order to secure the release of our sailors. One way or the other he lied. I conclude that the test of necessity is both vague and vagrant and that each of us should limit its use as much as possible in order to enlarge the areas in which the righteousness of the voluntary community may come into play.

Previously I have proposed that the government of our country as a last resort assume the responsibility now of taking care of the physical and mental needs of our people when the family and the church are unable to. Now I voice my hope that our government will leave these needs of the other peoples of the world unattended to except when the interests of national defense require it. Only after a world government becomes viable can our government hope to join effectively in fulfilling these needs. I recognize that this distinction in the treatment of our peoples and the other peoples of the world is arrogant and arbitrary even though probably constitutionally sound. My support of mandatory aid for our people but not of our mandatory aid for the poor of the world constitutes a compromise I arrive at in the hope of attracting to the search for the kingdom those who demand that our government do so much in the name of justice. Maybe our country has the resources and the governmental structures to take care of its own in the so-called name of justice. But as for the rest of the world, we have neither the resources nor the governmental structures to take care of all. Here the first need is for a world government. To those of you who believe the above-mentioned compromise of mine stretches necessity too far from what is right, I beg your forgiveness. It may well be that it is never necessary for any government to adopt these social welfare programs, or it may be that it is necessary for a government to adopt such programs only after the companion voluntary community has achieved some semblance of oneness. By this I mean an integrated voluntary community as opposed to a pluralistic society. In any event, all of you will understand my own feeling that the times required me to make this compromise. "The Great Society" has not yet been humbled.

Let us now return to our discussion of how the farmer produces food to fulfill man's basic physical need therefor. We have seen how in an open marketplace the farmer ought to be able to fill this need with very little help from government or any voluntary community, provided he does not meet with misfortune and provided the consumers, through employment or investments, have the required purchasing power. We have also seen how the farmer can try to protect himself against crop failures through savings, insurance, and investment, all carried out in an open marketplace, with very little need for help from government or any voluntary community. We now will look at personal misfortunes that the farmer or any other worker may encounter. Personal tragedy may be self-inflicted, but more likely it will occur from catastrophic accident. Self-inflicted misfortune, such as a minor case of indolence or a major case of drug abuse, may ultimately be preventable, primarily through faith and education offered by the voluntary community, but catastrophes I fear will always be with us. Let us focus, therefore, on the worker who, savings exhausted, finds himself without a job or with a medical disability.

The problem of training those willing and able to work to learn a job or a new job presently is handled by both public and private sectors. During the transition from unemployment to employment currently there are often available three types of governmental programs: subsidized training programs, unemployment compensation, and welfare. We suggest that without much imagination but with great effort the private sector could soon take over these programs.

The problem of health care is an enormously more difficult one. Because of the fantastic costly scientific advances in the healing arts, the rich today have available miraculous cures. In our democracy the demanding expectations of all the people for indiscriminate attention and equal treatment dramatize the problem. Some of these medical procedures are so expensive that if the patient were to bear all their costs his bill could exceed in amount the total lifetime earnings of a laborer. As any fair government should treat all of its people without discrimination, and as this is not, and is not about to be, possible in the furnishings of health care, itself another Aesop's fable, my unappealing solution is to get government out of this act as quickly as possible by letting the churchly aspect of the voluntary community take it over now. Death and sickness are facts of life. Healing is one of Jesus' priorities, but interfering with God's will can take place in this as in other endeavors. The church is best equipped to determine how much Frankenstein should enter into this process of prolonging life, not only from the standpoint of suggested standards for people to follow, but also from that of striking a compassionate balance between the requests for voluntary contributions from the community and the furnishing of these life-prolonging procedures to the needy without charge. I would far rather leave these matters to the judgment of the pope than to the decisions of the courts. Do you not find unsightly the vast expenditure of public funds used to support the prolonging of life through man's inventions and contrivances while at the same time public funds are used to deny life through abortions? Does it not almost look as though man is trying to show God who's boss?

There is another dimension to the problems posed by misfortunes affecting workers. Many of these misfortunes, whether self-inflicted or accidental, have man-made causes. Consider, as an example, drug abuse. Whether you consider it a sickness or a self-inflicted disability, the fact is it would not be possible without a supplier, by which term I include everybody involved, grower through trafficker to dealer on the street corner. This brings us to a discussion of crime and punishment.

In the transition from a mandatory to a voluntary community, the last vestige of government will be the punishment of crime in order that law and order may be maintained. Long after the coming of our world government and the disappearance of wars and armies, the police force will remain necessary. I feel helpless in the presence of only two types of people, the insane and the felons. Gladly I leave the insane (provided not criminally insane) to the custody of the voluntary community, but the felon who diminishes his fellowman frightfully or totally must be put away. If society can afford it, I have no objection to imprisonment for as long as life in appropriate cases, to parole for good behavior in appropriate cases, to a prison environment that allows self-education if the environment is austere, and to visitation by priests or others whose purpose is to keep kindled the spirit of the criminal. I do not even voice any complaint to the death penalty in capital cases. I do not ask for it or favor it, however, as it is against my principles and desires and neither my safety nor my sense of justice or of retribution requires it. I am against rehabilitation programs for prisoners because of my belief, expressed throughout this book, that mandatory government can do no good, especially in such a compulsory spirit-smothering setting. So much for him who willfully destroys another's spirit totally or nearly so.

The drug supplier falls somewhere in between the murderer and prohibition's moonshiner or smuggler and should be treated accordingly. Every deterrent short of the death penalty itself should be brought into play to destroy the product at its source and throughout its movement and to stifle those involved at every step of the way. Note how the problem of drug abuse vividly exemplifies the proper way to tackle any antisocial problem—not by invoking the aid of government in a scattergun approach over the entire scene, but by having each of our two communities do what each does best, the government emphasizing the negative, the law, and the voluntary community the positive, the spirit, the government telling the supplier he cannot support the user's habit, the voluntary community aiding the addict to realize he can kick the habit.

Thus ends our consideration of the farmer and his problems. He has served us well in enabling us to analyze proper functions of our two communities in the present real world and the future ideal world and in portraying problems of all producers. As production and distribution are the major concerns of economics, we proceed to get the farmer's food to market. This chapter now ceases to be a tour de force on the above-mentioned functions and becomes a hasty potpourri of flourishes upon these underpinnings.

Distribution requires transportation. Customarily cargo is transported by ships at sea, shipments are transported by freight cars on railroad tracks or by trucks on land, and freight is transported by planes in the air. Today water and air transportation are primarily and properly carried out with minimal governmental regulation. I would like to see rail service, both passenger and freight, taken over by the private sector under exclusive grants of monopoly to several geographically separated carriers, for reasons comparable to those already advanced in support of private water companies. We cannot afford competing rail rights of way, because our need for land is at such a premium. I have a hunch that the solution to today's air traffic congestion eventually will be likewise to grant exclusive monopolies over avenues of air space. At this time I cannot see the national highway system, any more than city streets, other than as they are now, under the control and responsibility of the appropriate governmental unit. In time I believe each unit could contract out this responsibility for building and maintaining the highways to independent contractors, as many do today.

The passage of the farmer's products to the consumer through other steps in the distribution process, including, in addition to transportation, services of processors, wholesalers, and retailers, would appear to pose few extraordinary problems that a free and open marketplace can not handle. Similarly, the passage of other raw materials from producer to consumer, such as clothing, in satisfaction of man's physical needs, would probably, if taken independently, follow an analysis much like that we have taken for food.

Shelter, however, involves real estate and presents a tough problem of location. Houston, the last I knew, had no zoning laws. Except for the absence of graffiti, I have always felt the town looked like hell, especially when one considers how much money has gone into its buildings. Admittedly, Houston has several attractive business enclaves built in the tradition of the inwardly oriented Spanish home. This brings up one of my prejudices. I have always found provocative the difference between the English and the Spanish view of what constitutes a fine home. The outer solid stone walls of the Spanish home face the street. The rooms, windows, and most doors all look out upon a beautiful floral inner courtyard. The English cottage, on the other hand, is built in the center of a floral yard. Its rooms and windows with their geranium flower boxes all look out over the rolling green countryside.

But prejudice aside, although I believe the absence of zoning laws contributes to Houston's hodgepodge, I doubt that zoning laws are the panacea. Most PUDs (Planned Urban Developments) remind me of a bunch of chicken coops. My company was about the second entrepreneur to acquire one of the last remaining large landholdings on Philadelphia's main line. We were not able to develop it because of the excessive demands of the township's planning experts and the elaborate zoning requirements for a first-class development. After us, several other developers also failed. I believe one went to jail for cutting corners. Today the beautifully rolling tract with its large Victorian manor house has been denuded and replaced with clusters, numerous large, ugly wooden clusters of papier-mâché, expensive two- and four-family townhouses, each built as though in an attempt to be a replica of the old manor house and each looking out at each other, jowl to jowl over limited air space separated by the planner's occasional sparse stand of a few trees. From the air I am reminded of the hobnails on the sole of Paul Bunyan's boot.

Of the gourmet's excess in fine foods and of the fashionmonger's excess in fine clothing I say *de gustibus non disputandum,* provided the government protects rare wild creatures as in the past they protected salmon, alligators, and egrets and as they continue to protect such furbearers as seals and leopards. Perhaps these excesses might be treated under the subject of values in an educational program sponsored by the voluntary community. They do not require significant governmental activity. But man's desire for fine homes and for fine office buildings is different. This desire feeds upon land, which man cannot make. All he can do is control its use. I agree that it is nice to have in our towns and cities areas set aside for residential development, other areas for commercial development, and still others for industrial development and to have such uses enforced at this time by zoning laws. I do not agree, however, that I should be taxed as I am for the salaries of all the city planners, art commissioners, and other boards, for all their scatterbrained visions of convention centers, coliseums, and a new Atlantis, and for all the messy litigation the ensuing conflicts over property rights entail. I am going to let you work out your own balance of what force is necessary in handling these concerns, as I believe our society is excessively housebound.

There were an Englishman and a Persian, both remembered for only one thing, the former's translation of the latter's poem. The poet's view of sex was right on. Note how the pope and I, and maybe others, think sex is a good place to start developing one's values. Anyway, we all know the verse: "a jug of wine, a loaf of bread, and thou beside me singing in the wilderness." That poet's view of shelter was also right on: a beautiful campsite under the stars and a different one each night. My homes have provided me adequate lodging, but not the nights I remember. Last summer there was the night the tent was pitched over moose tracks on a great lake's sandy beach, while with "thou" camping by canoe in solitude in La Vérendrye, just a long day's drive from Philadelphia. Last winter there were similar nights in Florida's Everglades. Imagine trying to sleep listening to tarpon feeding beside you when all you can see are red eyes of alligators. Years ago in a high Rocky Mountain cirque there was the night made sleepless by the caterwauling of a cougar as he circled our protective small Indian-type camp fires, crazed by the aroma of steaks a group of us kids had stupidly packed in, cooked, and gorged ourselves on that night. Later there was the sleep startlingly interrupted when first we heard the maniacal calls of the loon. We still have torn tent netting as a reminder of my fitful attempt while still unawake to escape what sounded like encircling werewolves. Still later there was the morning in Joe Buckskin Gulch with the little ones after our first family climb of a fourteen-thousander when, opening the tent flap, we saw six inches of the season's first snowfall, which during the night had left everything a beautifully forbidding white. Just the day before there had been beautifully inviting spruce forests with one lonely stand of bristlecone pine until we had come to timberline and the easy walk up the red rock to the top. No, give me a home of my own with room to eat, sleep, read, write, entertain a few friends, and stow my gear, in peace, and a peaceful office downtown, and I will let the city planners worry about God's hang-up over man's monuments, as reported in Genesis.

This completes our discussion of the fulfillment of man's physical needs. In earlier chapters we have shown ways to fulfill man's mental needs and man's spiritual needs. Accordingly, our last concern with the mandatory community is how to protect and maintain our government while we yet need it. In Benjamin Franklin's words: "You have a republic. Let us see if you can keep it." One way to keep it is to protect it from outside enemies. Enough has been said about the threefold approach to this protection. It consists of (1) a strong defense; (2) the pursuit of a world government; and (3) the attempt in every endeavor to help outside enemies become friendly.

Another way to keep the republic is to protect it from inside enemies. The actual inside enemies are the criminals. We have already seen how it is more difficult to help them become friendly because they are in our midst. For our safety they cannot be left free from our restraints as are our outside enemies. Yet once you shackle the body you cannot enjoy the benefits of dealing with an unshackled spirit. What you can do, however, is nip off potential criminals in their budding by either changing the depraved environments or getting the kids out of such environments. Until our first two institutions, families and voluntary community, become more responsible in fulfilling these tasks, which they should be doing right now, government may have to step in. Even after compulsory universal free public education is abolished, I see a continuing need to force kids in these neighborhoods to go to special governmental schools during their formative years.

Another way to keep the republic is not to overburden it. How open should our society be? How free from immigration and emigration restrictions? Presently I see no problem in our current policy of letting our people go, but I question our immigration policy. Ours is a society that, whether you like it or not, aims, one way or another, to have each of us take care of all of us from cradle to grave. Prudence necessitates our not inflating the "all" with indigents through loose immigration laws or otherwise. So when I reflect upon the high birthrates of our own indigent populations the logic of necessity pushes me compellingly and remorselessly to the final dirty expedient of domestic government, education in safe sex, safe sex, the ultimate expression of the not to be, of the denial of life itself.

I can hardly believe I have made this last recommendation, I whose views of polity were fueled by Ayn Rand, Frank Chodorov, and Frederich Hayek, "root, hog, or die," "laissez-faire." Their libertarian views are entirely consistent with Christianity. They would have government do nothing but maintain the peace and let the individual help the needy. Their attitude is a step in the right direction on the road to the kingdom. The only thing wrong with it is that it will not work today. It is a step whose time has not yet come. Its equation misses an important element. It ignores the serpent, and he demands attention. So let us once again hear from him.

Most men are pushy bastards who will not stand idly by and let government do nothing when all about them they see crucial social evils. After all, Jesus (voluntary community) commanded his followers to transform the world, and democracy (mandatory community) commands its citizens to elect candidates who will serve all people equally—both exceedingly pushy commands. In the depression people squealed at me, "You just cannot let people starve." Today others are squealing at me, "You just cannot let people kill unborn babies." Both groups are compulsive do-gooders who have to impose their views on others. Hence, as we cannot change the pushiness of man, let us see if we can create a procedure or framework that slowly may be able to eliminate any need for it.

Individuals who do good voluntarily using their own resources, those whom T. S. Eliot and, I am sure, others have called the innocents, no-harmers etymologically speaking, represent the flip side of the wise and the prudent who rely on serpentine wisdom. Today, without the steadying structure of the law, the harmless exercises of the innocents can easily become as futile as those of pearl casters or as self-destructive as those of undisciplined children. So the serpentine trick here is this: just as the parent furnishes a steadying discipline for the child so that the child's activities are neither wasteful nor self-destructive and then slowly relaxes such discipline as the child matures in wisdom, so let society use the steadying influence of mandatory government, trying at all times, however, to relax it as it becomes unnecessary. We will not now be able, and so we will not even try, to convince any compulsive do-gooder that any short-term "good" he may accomplish through use of the force of government is far outweighed by the long-term spiritual destruction he causes. We can, and so I hope we shall, ask him to test his proposed activity against the appropriate standard: when the objective can be attained by people working together using friendly persuasion without the force of government, then pursue the objective if it is good; when the objective requires the force of government, then pursue the objective if it is necessary; but do not confuse the two. For those obstinate self-righteous do-gooders who insist upon continuing to do so we have reserved the eleventh exit.

Remember, it is absolutely never necessary to do good. If it is necessary then it is not goodness. For to do good is to follow the will of God, what one believes to be the right, of one's own volition without any compulsion of anyone, even of one's self, and without imposing one's will upon another. It is also absolutely never good to do what is necessary. If it is good then necessity has nothing to do with it. You've heard the awkward comment made by the embarrassed gift recipient: "How awfully good of you, but it really wasn't necessary for you to go to all the bother." For to do what is necessary is to invoke the law that restricts and rules and in so doing denies the spirit. That this is not sophism may be more easily seen perhaps if I use a more vulgar word than *necessary,* as *necessary* has an abstract overtone of nonexistence. I suggest the word *expedient* as a substitute. Remember how in an early chapter I pointed out that all institutions necessarily somewhat diminish their members and how by definition an institution is where the members all stand in it together. Well, when we want to pull our foot out of it, to *ex pedis,* we are being expedient, but you would not call it being good.

Reducing the number of indigents is only one of the many ways to avoid overburdening our republic in an attempt to save it. I used this way as the example that, though cruel, best portrays the thesis of this book. Senator Proxmire, over the years he was in office, regularly gave Golden Fleece awards for sad examples of ludicrous wastes of millions of taxpayers' dollars. In the next edition of this book I hope to enumerate these awards, because facts support a thesis far better than theory and the impact of such a list would be awesome. Probably the overburdening, however, that most endangers the republic arises when blocs of voters try, through governmental programs, to have others than themselves contribute in providing them with amenities of life that can not properly be called necessities. I am thinking of the Roman circuses of the day, lotteries, sports stadia, convention centers, music halls, art museums, and primarily the many other activities that fall under the heading of services in general, most of which activities to the extent a society desires them voluntary communities have always been able to provide. These "services," with few exceptions, can never meet any test of necessity. If people need food, let it be said and as the last resort let government provide food. If the complaint is that governmental services are being discontinued, let us know which ones. More often than not the one who is complaining is not the one served, but the one who in providing the alleged service will lose a government job sucking off the taxpayers' tit.

George Washington said, "Government is not reason. It is not eloquence. It is force! Like fire, it is a dangerous servant and a fearful master." Do you think the fire of government is well contained today? In the chapter on the family we witnessed the continuing struggle between the parents' guidance and the child's spirit and the continuing danger of a loss of balance between these two ingredients that if carefully blended will ultimately and hopefully result in the maturing of a new adult capable of self-guidance. Since that chapter we have been portraying the continuing struggle between governmental guidance and the spirit of a society as reflected in its voluntary institutions and the continuing danger of a loss of balance between these two ingredients that if carefully blended now may ultimately and hopefully result in the maturing of a society capable of self-guidance without the fiery force of government. Do I think the fire of government is well contained today? In no way. Our society is about as mature as a spoiled brat who has not yet learned to walk, and our government's overbearing paternalism is about to consume the spirit of our society. But until the end there always remains hope, so let's get on with it.

Here is our dream. I see the glorious day when all mankind realize that some man's pushing his fellowman around is the cause of all public problems and that loving kindness without compulsion is the only righteous relationship between men. Until that day reasonable men are going reasonably to differ on the handling of public problems, so I look forward to an earlier day when public problems still requiring relationships between men based upon compulsion, whether manifested in its most physically and spiritually ugly form as war or obscured in an ugly manner under the guise of law, will be addressed in this fashion: the compulsion shall be invoked only after a reasonable time has been spent unsuccessfully in finding noncompulsory solutions and then only after carefully weighing the seriousness of the immediate problem and the likelihood of the compulsion affecting a temporary solution against the seriousness of the additional public problems that such compulsion will certainly produce from what might be described as the long-lived backlashing effect. Just read Old Testament history and see how it describes exactly what is happening around Jerusalem today if you want a good example of the longevity of the backlash.

Now let me dramatize this dream from yet another perspective. Shakespeare was a piker when he said, "If you want a better world, kill all the lawyers''; he should have said, ''Kill all the leaders,'' a task we shall proceed to accomplish in the next chapter.

Chapter XII
On Service

Our goal of philosophical anarchy has been before us. Next came the method to be used to attain this goal, what may be called the ways and the means. The purpose of this short pornographic chapter is to dramatize through sexual imagery the thought that the way is not to be found through leadership.

One summer when I was a member of the university's guide service a lady casually asked me while we were waiting to start a tour what I was studying to become. I replied with instant sophomoric integrity, "A leader."

"A leader," she mused aloud. Her next question was: "If you all study to become leaders, who will be the followers?"

I still remember my conceited, weak smile, which left this question rhetorical. Each of us should lead only himself and resist in others all other forms of leadership except that which is absolutely necessary for the welfare of the three vital communities of family, church, and, temporarily, state.

Let us start with one of Shakespeare's keen couplets that reveals the devilish integrity of its speaker:

> For conscience is a word that cowards use,
> Devised at first to keep the strong in awe.

Let us paraphrase this couplet in order to introduce the subject of this chapter:

> For service is a word that leaders use,
> Devised at first to keep the pack in line.

Service will not be eulogized in this book. Philosophical anarchy is not attainable through service. The word *service* has been too overworked, and too frequently incorrectly or ambiguously used, for it to be of any use.

Service, like *servant,* is a correlative word, and both derive their meaning from the "master," the recipient of the service, the one for whose benefit or at whose command the work, the service, is performed. As there is only one Lord and Master, service to another is sacrilege. Such sacrilege often takes the form of serfdom or sex. When it takes the form of serfdom, the master-servant relationship can easily become ambiguous. Consider how big-business activity today is changing from manufacturing businesses to financial services. In manufacturing the servants produced a tangible, visible end product for the manufacturer. But in financial servicing the exercise often results in loss of the original investment and causes one to wonder whether the parties had not forgotten our Lord's frequent admonition that the servant is never greater than the master.

When servicing another involves sex, the master-servant relationship really gets dicey. The Philadelphia lawyer who was my preceptor felt very sorry for his colleague who had to humor his client and neighbor, a rich farmer, by bartering bills for services rendered each year. The lawyer's bill was for his routine legal services; the farmer's bill was for services rendered by his bull to the lawyer's cows. I might add that my preceptor's sorrow never interfered with his enjoyment in telling this story. Laughter aside, though, who is to say who is the servicer and who the master in the human mating act? Who is serving whom? Avoiding having to answer this question in order to keep peace in the family may be reason enough for giving up on the word *service.* I am reminded of the punch line in the limerick about the disputatious lesbians and gays from Khartoum who wasted their days in seeking the ways who does what and with which and to whom. Whenever one asks you to serve, or whenever one asks you to let him serve you, serpentine wisdom prompts you to inquire who is on the giving end and who is on the receiving end.

Incidentally, I owe to an egotistical minister my unraveling of the limerick's dilemma. Unlike the pope, who is *servus servorum Dei* (servant of the servants of God), this minister had the temperament of a submagistrate and like the dominies of yesteryear perceived himself as a thorn who needled people, citing St. Paul's goad. This prompted me to write the following poem. I remembered that the Romans of St. Paul's day, in taking an oath, placed their hands not on a Bible, but on their testicles—what better witnesses to a man's activities and what better reason, according to the etymologist, for a lady's demanding orchids?

Blinding Insight on the Road to Damascus

The ear is to hear
The arm to harm
The testis to attest
Testicles and prickles
Eyewitnesses and blind witnesses
The prick to Paul
Jehovah's witnesses
The balls of God

Voilà. There is the means to our end. By self-leadership we will witness rather than serve, and we will subject to the test of necessity all the stuff that spews forth from the shakers, the movers, the pushers, the take-chargers, and all the other little pricks who while professing to serve others really want others to serve them. Their need for a piece of the action reminds one of the way yearling rams-to-be in the spring jump up on the old ewe's back and immediately fall off.

I shall conclude this pornographic interlude with a religious appeal to what the parlor folk will consider to be a more acceptable part of the body to invoke as a witness and with results probably no more successful than Barry Goldwater's similar invocation. It was several millennia ago that the prophet Jeremiah revealed God's new covenant. God told Jeremiah that deep within the people he would plant his law, writing it in their hearts. Then he would be their God and they his people. There would be no further need for one to tell another to learn to know God and his law: "No, they will all know me, the least no less than the greatest."

Chapter XIII

More about a Voluntary Community

We leave mandatory government and return to a voluntary community. It is fitting that our last specific suggestion for governmental action was education in safe sex, because in emphasizing what is necessary it dramatizes the difference between these two communities. We leave the necessary bad and return to the realm of righteousness, innocence, and purity, purity as pure as the procreation that sex is all about. In making this transition we now tackle the toughest assignment for this book. We know we want the voluntary community to take over the functions of the mandatory community, but how and when? We believe the process will be evolutionary, a function at a time. But when, O serpent? What should be our time schedule? The serpent cannot answer these questions. The poor serpent never did have any sense of timing. Watch this.

We are seeking God's kingdom by trying, as Jesus commands us, to be perfect like God himself. Well, if this is the end, is it not exactly where the serpent put Eve in the first place? He told her, "Eat the apple and be a god!" For this reason man should only be concerned with the means. The end is in the hands of God. In this truth lies an indirect message to all the bottom-liners of the world from the serpent, the original bottom-liner par excellence.

So the purpose of this chapter is to reveal the means by which, once the mandatory community gives up its sovereignty over some aspect of life, a voluntary community may take up the slack without asserting sovereignty. I appreciate that securing a universal voluntary community will be even harder than dispensing with the mandatory community. The universal requirement increases the difficulty, but it is needed for cohesion and it is not without precedent.

Indeed, there is probably not an original idea in this book. I am innovator, not inventor. All I am doing is taking partially accepted ideas and putting them together novelly. For example, there have been over the years many voluntary religious-oriented communities that have emphasized the holy spirit's guiding each man without the need for church rule. I have heard unchurched Lincoln quoted as having said, "God always lets me know what he wants me to do." This is more than I can say. The problem is that whenever such a group tries to do its thing and make an impact on the world its disorderliness proves divisive and eventually destroys it. One has to work through the universal institutions. The Roman church proclaims such universality in her theory and in our country boasts in practice a membership of over 53 million, almost a quarter of our population, so it is the obvious vessel for our community.

Once again, therefore, our structure is in place. Conceptually the transition from mandatory to voluntary community appears to be clean and concise. Society need not change drastically. The change may occur a little at a time over decades or centuries almost imperceptibly, as when today the private sector, unnoticed, takes over some governmental function. Ultimately, however, a free and open marketplace subject to the standard of righteousness will handle the fulfillment of the physical needs of most people. The church will care for the unfortunates, supplying them with food, clothing, and shelter. What were matters formerly governed by laws will become matters voluntarily accepted as habits, such as traffic codes, contributions instead of taxes, services like fire fighting and trash collections, grants of monopoly, or other matters where the continuing spirit of the laws is required. The church will take over education with the secular option available to all as described in chapter 6. The church will provide spiritual leadership and proclaim the standard of righteousness in all matters. The church will have no powers of enforcement but only of moral suasion.

What I am asking the church to do is something it has never done before. I ask it not to withdraw from the world, as did much of the Lutheran church in Hitler's Germany. I ask it not to try to transform the world governmentally, as did our southern Baptists in foisting prohibition upon us. I ask it not to be above the world, with its spiritual lords matching the lords temporal in power, as has Rome throughout most of its history. All I ask is that it be above the world, proclaiming the standard of righteousness for all voluntarily to follow, and that it have pastors like shepherds who take care of the flock that needs their care. Just as people will voluntarily accept traffic signals, so everyone in the world will voluntarily accept these shepherds, even though they will be appointed by the hierarchy. Although this authoritative practice may strike one as very undemocratic, I support it in my innocence with the slogan "it takes one to know one" and in my serpentine wisdom with this anecdote that reveals how Machiavelli might view the democratic way a congregation of my church currently selects its minister.

The background for this anecdote is that Niccolò Machiavelli, the secretary of state for the Florentine republic at the turn of the fifteenth century, lost his position when the Medici took over that republic, failed to get a comparable position from the new rulers even though in retirement he wrote for them a brilliant book on how to handle their new job, and before long thereafter was signing his letters to a friend: "Ambassador to the Minor Friars, J.U.D.," which caused me to wonder: what is this gifted little scoundrel up to now? Well, it seems that the hierarchy of that day was so busy ruling both church and state they had little time for pastoral matters and so had appointed him to be the search committee for a new padre for the local parish.

For those who may not know, a search committee, as I have seen it, operates in this fashion. First, they circulate to the membership a fifteen-odd-page multiple choice questionnaire. Under the heading "Personality" they may ask you to list in order of your preference various traits for the priest to have, such as: dynamic speaker, good preacher, personal warmth, good administrator, good listener, good character, good counselor, good pastor, committed Christian, educated in Scripture, et cetera. Under the heading "Social Action" you may be asked whether you wish him to take positions on all issues, some issues, or no issues, all of the time, some of the time, or none of the time. One question I remember in particular was: "If you dislike anything about church, check whom you would tell: your family, the minister, the vestry, other members of the congregation, anybody, nobody?" Then the responses are all put into the computer and out comes a parish profile, which is matched up against the profiles kept in the diocesan office of available priests. Thus armed, the committee starts searching while the bishop says, "God knows who is going to be the new priest; all the search committee needs to do is pray."

The world knows how Machiavelli advised the prince to act (*prince* means "temporal ruler," what we would call king), but I doubt that it knows how he advised himself to act as search committee sole. He wrote: "As all our past priests have had one or another of the deadly vices I am going to find one who has them all so that by seeing all evil we will be led to good." Incidentally, J.U.D., the degree Machiavelli conferred upon himself, is the only honorary degree I would accept for writing this book, namely, Juris Utriusque Doctor (doctor of both laws, civil and canon).

Can you not easily see how Machiavelli could find our current practice to be most authoritative? The committee sees itself as choosing a spiritual leader for the flock. They may take eighteen months, far less than the time it takes us to elect a secular leader, namely, our president. So the bishop compassionately relieves them of this great, burdensome responsibility by telling them the new priest has already been chosen. Implicit, though, is the requirement to follow the bishop's suggestion.

Finally, participation of the people in the voluntary community, although hopefully very active, may be no more than each wishes, provided he makes his voluntary contributions.

I know Rome has a long way to come before she can serve as a model for such a voluntary community, primarily because she does not understand the importance of the separation of church and state and the importance of the difference between the proclamation and the enforcement of dogma. Although I can sympathize with the pastor who at times feels he must discipline his flock as a father disciplines his children, if Rome wants to be our voluntary community she must give up her sanctions. For with sanctions there would merely be a substitution of one form of mandatory community for another, a substitution of an ayatollah for a government under law. We must never forget that a cruel religious ruler is far and away history's worst example of *Homo sapiens*.

But even after the hierarchy gives up its mandatory ways, it will take time before it is able to digest the vast assignment of secular homework I have given it throughout this book. Remember how we got here. If the spirit of man is to thrive in a voluntary community undiminished by compulsions of law, each of us will have to replace the external discipline of government with the internal discipline of self-restraint. Self-discipline presumes sufficient knowledge of the subject matter to know when such discipline is required. Just as I have wished that the pope could speak authoritatively about the financial markets, genetic splicing, and the ozone hole, as I certainly do not know enough to, so our voluntary community will require a process for translating the general test of what is right into a pragmatic specific suggestion as to what should be done with respect to all of the problems of life. Philosophers can contribute mightily to this process, but I doubt they have sufficient missionary zeal to direct it. Plato can deify beauty, truth, and goodness. The university can ever search for truth. But just to look for the truth does not lead to action and hard decision making. So I look to Rome to supply us with position papers on all the issues of the day. That is the homework to which I have just referred.

I also know that the rest of Christendom will have an even further way to come before it can join a voluntary community under the leadership of Rome and, of course, the non-Christian world would have the furthest way to come. Moreover, what adds to the difficulty is that we do not have a wheel to use to reach our objective. The ecumenical wheel has not yet been invented. Oh, I know about the so-called ecumenical movement in Protestant denominations, which seeks an accommodation, a rapprochement, with Rome. But these efforts, like those of universal hegemonies of the past, from Alexander the Great and before down through the Pax Britannica and after, are centered in unifying power and have no relevance whatever to Christ's kingdom. The clerics deplore their lack of sanctions to enforce a terrific drive to do good. They deplore the ineffectiveness of groups such as the National Council of Churches. In short, they want power.

For example, my denomination, after talking with Rome for years and after conceding liturgical practices and local autonomy, is down to one major obstacle to reunion, to wit, Rome's unwillingness to accept our married priests and our female priesthood. If in a mandatory community the standard of necessity prompted the Protestant Bourbon to say Paris was worth a mass, then in a voluntary community the standard of righteousness should certainly prompt any priest to say the universal church is worth loss of a job. The direction of this ecumenical movement has been for an increase in the power and authority of the church, whereas the proper direction should be for a increase in local autonomy and liturgical freedom.

At the time I wrote the above remarks about the ecumenical movement I intentionally omitted mention of the Orthodox branch of the Holy Catholic Church, because I knew nothing to say about it. But my current reading has just tickled my imagination to conceive a wildly exciting idea, which I shall now share with you. First, I must point out that I read books as lawyers read cases. We try to find support for our position. We try to find a prior case in which the facts were exactly the same as the facts in our pending case and in which the judge in the prior case reached the decision we would like the judge to reach in our case. Rarely are you fortunate enough to find such a case "on all fours." Second, I have just read *The Brothers Karamazov,* because it is one of the so-called great books and, incidentally, because I hoped to see whether it contained anything to refresh my recollection of where in my past I had ever bumped into the concept of philosophical anarchy. I believe it was in *War and Peace,* but I doubt I will find the time to read that great book again, especially the last fifty pages, which I remember as being incomprehensible to me in the forties. Imagine my surprise when I found Dostoyevski had one of his characters, the learned monk Father Paissy, say:

> Understand the Church is not to be transformed into the State, that is Rome and its dream. That is the third temptation of the devil. On the contrary, the State is transformed into the Church, will ascend and become a Church over the whole world—which is the complete opposite of Ultramontanism and Rome— . . . [and is] the glorious destiny ordained for the Orthodox Church. This star will arise in the east!

Imagine my coming upon such a statement. Nothing could be more on all fours with my dream than that. Yet a mere thirty-seven years after Dostoyevski wrote this that star of his arose over the worst civilized and organized brutality the world had yet seen, and today, another seventy years later, that glorious ordained destiny remains dormant. Imagine this lawyer's predicament. I have just found a case on all fours in which the judge reached the diametrically wrong result, a dream comparable to mine that brought about the opposite of what was dreamt, a most unfortunate situation that would send any lawyer scurrying.

Now for the wildly exciting idea. I scurried, but I did not have to go far. Just a few days before, in reading a book on New Testament history I learnt that in taking the Gospel to Greece, which is considered the home base of the Orthodox church, St. Paul, who regarded himself as inwardly free from the law, had insisted that the Gentile Christians must not adopt the law of Moses. Paul's position was that with the coming of Jesus the law was not a means of salvation. Salvation was the free gift from God conferred by the spirit. When the Jewish Christians heard of this, they recalled Paul to Jerusalem and suggested he participate in a vow that the Jewish Christians need not forsake the law, and he did. May I attribute to this difference in the way Peter and Paul received the message of Jesus world communism's contempt for the law? After all, if the spirit alone is important, then if you don't have the spirit you have lost the battle and it doesn't much matter whether you act legally or illegally thereafter. May I think a great saint's boo-boo caused Russia's agony in my lifetime? If I may, then I have properly dreamt of a voluntary community in the hands of Rome. Rome can be counted on not lightly nor too quickly to relinquish the necessity of the law, but Rome can never fulfill my dream for her until she relinquishes the external manifestations of the law, because the kingdom will not come until the state is transformed into the church.

So although we have no wheel in place I believe we do not need to invent a new wheel, but only to blend together innovatively the vision of the kingdom that some religionists believe can be at hand here and now with the vision of the unruled society that some philosophers have already described. And as we approach the end of this book I must take one last crack at trying again to bring philosophers and theologians together to convince, with some new insights, thinkers and believers, the brightest and the best, to work together in seeking the kingdom.

Born a believer, I learned to suspend belief in order to think without destroying belief. Had I been born a philosopher, a lover of wisdom, I wonder if I ever could have suspended thought in order to believe. Like law, wisdom is a jealous mistress, but unlike a whore, wisdom is a goddess, Athena herself. I can see how the philosopher may well view me as a cad of the lowest order. I bitch incessantly about being pushed around by do-gooding bastards with respect to mere materialistic matters, yet I try to pervert his sacred mind and foist upon it "minimal unifying beliefs" for the good of the world. But try I must, because the wise and the good must work together if we are to find the kingdom.

So let the philosopher look ahead to a time when priest, prophet, and saint can join hands with philosopher, artist, and poet. Let him wonder if intuition, what one takes for granted rationally without applying reason or logic to it, may be the meeting place of faith and reason. And while friendly philosophers try to set up this meeting, let me in the spirit of compromise toss out to them two concessions and request from them only one in return. I will look forward to the day when the church withers away as an institution and remains solely as a temple where one may worship, praise, and give thanks to God, and I will agree in working for the kingdom in the real world not to mention the name of God; in return, they will receive my one superstition.

Just as we have contemplated the withering away of the institution of mandatory government, I see no reason why we cannot dare to envision the passing of the institutional church, provided this occurs only after all mandatory government has passed. But until the last vestige of government's dirty expediency has departed, the moral pressure of a strong church is required. Thereafter, I can visualize the faith being passed on from parent to child and the needy being cared for by foster parents and brothers' keepers. So much for my first concession.

My second concession to philosophers is a freebie for them, as I backed into it. The hearsay quotation I mentioned as coming from Lincoln disturbed me. I refer to the statement he allegedly made that he always knew what God wanted him to do. I shall have to verify it, as I have always liked him best of our presidents. This same thought appeared in our newspaper this past summer. The front page announced the retirement of a much-publicized local, gentle activist of good will who had brought about major unpopular changes in our society that today are generally accepted. In the interview he commented, "I always complained to God: 'Why do you make me do such things?' " In comparable vein, it is customary for political leaders to end their speeches invoking God's help for their programs. One recent president concluded a speech: "This is our course which we will follow with whatever help God may care to give us." As God is perfect and man is not, logically such loose chatter, such alienating self-righteousness, at some point is not going to reflect the will of God and is going to break the third commandment. So our next exit (#12) is for those who take the name of God in vain. Although I talk a lot about God—I have to, as I am trying to integrate religion and politics—you will remember that my stated motivation for writing this book was both vulgar and mundane: I want to be happy. Although later I added that I would not be writing this book unless I felt I were an apostle—that is, sent by God to do something—I have no idea whether or not it is the will of God that I write this book and I have never found "my calling." So I conclude it is better to leave mention of God out of the marketplace where political ideas are struggling for acceptance, struggles, justified only if necessary, that may reflect the will of God, but who is to say, and struggles that never reflect the way of God as revealed through the way of Jesus.

Here is the one concession I ask of the philosophers in return. Let us all accept my one superstition. Here are the steps. I find all institutions to be diminishing to the person, all committees and political group activities to be the embodiment of Prescott's "tedium of captivity," so much so that my opening word picture for any institution was, as the root of this word implies, the place where all stand in it together. At times have you not felt the same? Is it not natural, then, to want to stand above all this shit? You can do that with superstition. That is what the word means. But we want one unifying superstition. So let us all put our faith in the triune God, creator, Jesus, and holy spirit, and renounce all other superstitions, myths, icons, idols, gnosticisms, agnosticisms, egoisms, rights, democratic processes, or whatever else you may cherish as your superstition *du jour*.

The time has now arrived for us to reach the last exit on the highway to the kingdom. In the hope you will want to take the least traveled path, I shall summarize what these exits are all about and for whom I have mapped them. I want the idealistic kids who go to college after I am gone to have the benefit of a vision that I did not have. Put another way, we will always have rich, poor, and middle class, those rich in talents, financial or gifted abilities, poor in wealth, health, or gifted abilities, and the great middle class, the plodders, those who can get A's only for effort. It is for this silent majority that this book, written by one of their own, may have value and bring a breath of freedom like that the pacifist evangelist Henry Hitt Crane, pastor of the First Methodist Church in Scranton in the early thirties, brought me. I deprecate neither the rich nor the poor. The poor have more than they can handle with their own problems. The rich have so much going for them that they, impatient with the slowness of others, cut corners, but unfortunately for them, the way is straight and narrow. We plodders are the ones who can carry out the vision and profit from a briefing of the exits, because in life these exits come upon us faster than poorly marked exits on the expressways, so fast as to leave us confused as to which way is the straight and narrow way. No purpose is served by evaluating the most traveled exits, because the challenge is lost for him who gets off and stays off even if he gets off at the least traveled exit. It may be helpful, though, to list here the exits we have already discerned in tackling secular problems, namely, the exits for the faithless, the pushers, the irresponsible, the lazy, those who confuse, the intimidators, those who have excuses, the fearful, the legalists, the money grubbers, and the do-gooders.

In tackling the problems of a voluntary community the exits are of a different nature as the way becomes more difficult and demanding. Now even little things count much. I remember a pep talk Dr. Crane gave my senior class at high school. "If you want a better world," he said, "make sure everything you say is kind, thoughtful, and true." How such advice if followed would facilitate all problems of communication! Now we are dealing with the harmlessness of the dove more than with serpentine wisdom. So here we find exits for the unkind, the untruthful, the unthoughtful, and the unfair, as well as for the blasphemer, no matter how innocent. And here now we will discover our last exit, the exit for those who do not invoke the heavenly presumption in everything they do because as witnesses we proclaim in our every action that God is working his purpose out and we are seeking his kingdom. Perhaps now both you and I finally are ready to try to understand the story of the tower of Babel, the first story in the Bible that offended my mind. The story of the creation of the heavens and the earth in Genesis, for example, is neither illogical nor offensive. It is a beautifully poetic deified rendition of what even today some scientists say in fact could actually have taken place at the beginning. Let us now see if Babel is more than babble.

In one year's time the salesman's commissions had gone from the bottom in his agency to the top, and his manager asked him to what he attributed his success. His reply: "The one word they taught me to use in my course in communications skills."

"What was that word?"

"Fantastic."

The manager paused thoughtfully: "What word had you been using?"

"Bullshit."

In contrast, at college there prevailed the strong puritanical concept that if one had something worth saying the words would come out. Not surprisingly, the professor suggested to the lad who wanted a course in elocution that he might try Yale, which reportedly had a good school of drama.

After reflection, I suppose this is the point the stories of Babel and Pentecost, the New Testament counterpart, make, although both are troublesome. In Babel mankind in its early days decides to build a city and a tower to make a name for themselves lest they be scattered, an enterprise this commercial real estate lawyer would have encouraged, just as the earthly father encourages the child's early use of building blocks. Instead God prevented their doing so by then giving them all different languages to speak.

After the death of Jesus at the annual feast of Pentecost God gave the Galilean apostles the ability to speak in the differing tongues of all the peoples present.

The conclusion to be drawn from these two stories, I assume, is God will help us communicate when we are trying to follow his will and impede us when we are on a frolic of our own. In similar vein I suggest the first way to work for philosophical anarchy is to watch our everyday witnesses no matter how insignificant and when in doubt err in favor of looking to God, what I call invoking the heavenly presumption. Let me give you an extreme example.

After the excitement of the first five books of the Bible, I found the historical books of Joshua and Judges gruesome and boring, like TV violence. I came awake, however, in reading the last verse in Judges. The King James Version reads: "In those days there was no King in Israel: every man did that which was right in his own eyes." The New Jerusalem Bible, compiled by accredited present-day scholars, ends without footnote: ". . . every man did what he pleased." Note the difference. Is not the overtone of following the will of God stronger in doing what is right as one sees the right than in doing what gives one pleasure? I do not suggest the original be mistranslated, but if—and I do not know—the original is ambiguous, let us follow the translation that reflects what this book is about. Our last exit is for those who do not invoke the heavenly presumption.

So where does all this leave us? It has been two and a half years that I have enjoyed your unseen companionship in talking with you in the writing of this book. I hope you have enjoyed sharing my dream of a better world, because it is in the quest for a better world that I find meaning and purpose for life. I hope I have shown the paradoxical importance of the world's keeping its religious and political institutions entirely separate and at the same time of everyone's fulfilling the challenge of integrating his own religious and political thinking. This paradox requires the simultaneous use of two contradictory approaches: the voluntary religious or philosophical approach, involving groups open to all doing what is right and good in order to enable all to be all that they can be, and the mandatory political approach, involving governmental units doing what is necessary to hamper those who interfere with this voluntary approach and also doing what is necessary until the voluntary approach is effective. The religious institutions should be engrossed with the world as it should be, with the good, with the ideal, and with beauty and truth. Members of these communities participate in their activities voluntarily. On the other hand, the political institutions should be engrossed with the world as it is, with the necessary, with the real, and with ugliness and fraud. Members of these communities have to be kept together through force of arms or of laws. The more religion a society has, the greater is its faith. The less government a society has, the greater is its freedom. The greater the faith of a society and the greater its freedom, the better is the society. The religious and philosophical thinking provides its vision. The political thinking provides its pragmatism.

So what is my vision? What is my view of the promised land? It is a vision of a world without conflict, a vision of a world with self-government for everybody. This self-government is not democracy, because democracy consists of the imposition of the will of the active plurality upon everyone, what Plato called mob rule. The better form of government I offer, as a vision toward which to strive, is a world in which everyone governs only himself through a discipline taught in the family and the religious communities and through services provided under their auspices. As such a vision requires the cooperation of all, we religionists will have to broaden our appeal. We should deemphasize religious concern with what comes next and concern ourselves with how to follow the will of God in this world. And we must not have any dogmatic requirements for membership so as not to alienate cooperating freethinkers. Let me dramatize what I mean by such deemphasis. From A.D. 313, when Constantine established Roman Catholicism as the state religion, until 1920, when the pope signed the concordat with the Italian government, this numerically largest branch of Christendom was a theocracy, purporting from above to impose the will of God on this world and the next. It has only been since 1920 that the pope has agreed with the mandatory community that it is in charge of things temporal and that he is in charge of things spiritual. Thereby the church has further corrupted Mark Twain's corrupting epigram. Mark Twain, you remember, opined that the body is mortal and material and the soul is immortal and immaterial. Now the church leaves to Caesar what is mortal and immaterial while she handles what is immortal and material—everlasting life. (How much more immaterial can you get than to pass from dust to dust in a mere lifetime?) Would that the church concern itself with voluntary righteousness in this world and leave the next to the grace of God!

As I see it, our striving today to achieve a realization of this vision involves a pragmatic fourfold process:

1. *The creation of mandatory communities for societies that today lack a mandatory community:* This is the first step, because the law precedes the spirit in the civilizing process. The law shows us what is wrong. The laws are the parent's no-nos that give the child the framework in which his spirit finds its development. The learned lawyer's ability to understand the meaning of the expression *good faith,* only by contrast with its opposite, *bad faith,* reflects in miniature the transition from the Ten Commandments of the Old Testament to the good faith of the New Testament. We might call this process Peter's empowering of Paul. Today our most pressing need is for a mandatory world government. Without such, the world remains uncivilized. This is why I devoted one of the book's two chapters about mandatory government to the promulgation of a world constitution.
2. *The transfer to a voluntary community of as many of the mandatory activities as possible whenever any society thinks it has a viable mandatory community:* Timing is important here. When should each such transfer be made? I don't know the answer. There is no way to know for sure. Remember in our earlier discussion of the family the trouble we had in trying to decide how much parental law a child needs and how much freedom he should be allowed for the development of his spirit. One thing we did note. As the child gets older, the parental discipline must gradually wither away or the child's spirit will be destroyed. I suggest the same approach for the development of a society. In its primitive, uncivilized stage a society needs the law. After a society acquires the law, thereby becoming a mandatory community, and as it begins to feel civilized and grown-up, then that society must, like a parent, gradually begin to try

to let its people go by letting the private sector alone, so that the voluntary community, representing the spirit of the society, may develop. If the mandatory community does not gradually turn over its functions but instead tries to retain control of the maturing society by proliferating its laws to keep apace with the society's increasing sophistication, then the laws, like parental no-nos given to grown children, will suffocate the society's spirit and the society will drown in the whirlpools of Charybdis, disappearing from the face of the earth like civilizations of bygone years. This is why I devoted the second of the book's two chapters about mandatory government to thorough discussions showing how easily we could dispense with most of the governmental activities of our country.

3. *The development in each person of an attitude of reliance on and control over self in active obedience to an unknowable outside personal presence called God,* whose knowable standards, as knowable they must be to be obeyable, are derived from what we know about the man Jesus, in the absence of any other perfect man or woman about whom so much is known.
4. *Appreciation of the fact that so-called good people are as much a part of the problem as unfortunate or bad people:* The leader who encourages people to rely upon him and needs followers for his personal fulfillment is farther from achieving the proper attitude of self-reliance and self-control than the homeless who sleep on the city's steam vents in winter or the terrorists who violently seek to further their causes. We are called not to be leaders, but to be followers, followers not of ourselves or of any of us, but of something outside ourselves, as only then can we forget our divisions and work in unity.

* * * * *

I look forward to the day when all people will actively participate in this search for a better world, ever mindful, of course, that their first duties are to earn a living and engage in recreational activities. Let each one decide how much time should be devoted to acquiring bread and how much time to recreating, as reasonable men may reasonably differ on the respective values of these activities. For example, I suppose a gifted artist may properly devote his life to practicing and witnessing to others the inspirational expressions of his recreations. Or I suppose a competent entrepreneur may properly spend all of his life making jobs available in his business for those less competent or less interested in business endeavors. And I suppose a coal miner, without sophisticated equipment, may have to devote his leisure time solely to recreation in order to be able to brave the dirty darkness of the next day's work. But most people can find time, after work and recreation, for the search for the kingdom. Let each one also decide whether he is to contribute to the search working in the voluntary community or in governmental activity or in both, and let him decide what problems should be tackled by voluntary groups and what problems are within the proper domain of government, as reasonable men may reasonably differ on such matters also. No matter what form our involvement takes, following the advice of a dean of freshmen to the parents of the incoming class, let us be proud, supportive, merry, and wise.

Finally, let us not forget the twin banners that will lead us to victory, our standards of voluntary righteousness and mandatory necessity, for from these standards flow all of man's hopes for a better world. These are the starting points that the idealistic communists failed to find in 1917. The standard for the voluntary community to use is the test of righteousness. The voluntary approach will not be successful until there is a universal understanding and acceptance of what righteousness means. To say it means basic ethical norms such as honesty, nonviolence, promise keeping, free expression, and respect for person and property, such norms to be culled from the wisdom of the moral philosophers of the ages, is not sufficient. Such norms are too abstract, too relative, too contradictory, and too few. I find the meaning of righteousness in God's will for us as revealed by the Word, namely, by what Jesus of Nazareth is said to have said as written in the Gospels and as passed on from generation to generation by the Holy Catholic Church. You may propose a more concrete, more absolute meaning for the word *righteousness,* a meaning more susceptible of understanding and universal voluntary acceptance, but until you do, let us not reject our cornerstone.

The standard for the mandatory community to use is the test of what is necessary. The mandatory approach can never be successful because it is negative. Its compulsions favor some and harness others, so neither favored nor harnessed have any volition, any "being," in the situation. To the extent all are not free "to be" all that they can be, to that extent there can be no goodness, no righteousness. The standard for testing governmental activity is not what is good or right but rather what is necessary, because conceptually all governmental activity is wrong and bad. *Necessary* is the ideal word for this standard because its overtones exude negation. So let's hear the cry: Is this law really necessary? And let us patiently but ceaselessly try to educate those who scream, "You have to pass this law because it is right and just!" to see that they are part of the problem rather than helping in the search for the kingdom. Here is my last attempt to do so.

There are only two ways to look at man's law. Either you look at it as force and keep it at a minimum so that those of us who would like a better life for all people can voluntarily live on a higher moral plane. Or you look at it as justice and make it as all-encompassing as possible because what is there in life that should not be justly done. Justice, however, is not self-fulfilling. It requires laws. Laws require enforcers. All-encompassing laws require all-encompassing enforcers. Even then you have no assurance that the laws as enforced will do justice. Who enforces the enforcers? The taxes required to support such a bureaucracy of enforcers are so onerous that any taxpayer who complies without question with each jot and each tittle of the tax laws must take advantage of everything the law allows or risk extinction. Now the humanist, at first blush properly, says he would rather risk such extinction than risk my righteousness, which he views as allowing me with minimal legal restraints to exploit all for solely my own benefit. But my righteousness is pegged to God, whose spirit somehow works in me. My righteousness prompts my witness to God in my every deed. When one believes my witness is not directed toward a better life for all people, one may challenge me. And my God and my conscience motivate me to try my best to justify myself to you. You, too, have such a conscience. In every case conscience is self-enforcing. So I reply to the humanist: To follow my view that the law is a necessary evil admittedly is risky, but before you follow the view that the law is justice, please look where it is leading you. When you have to live up to the line of legality or risk extinction, you spend your time struggling with conflicting Aesop-fabled laws and with sluggish and often stupid bureaucrats. You spend your money on overburdening taxes. What happens is that legality replaces morality. I once heard a legalist pithily make this point. A religionist, who was sending his children to private school, was complaining because he was paying triply for their education—their tuition, ever-increasing school taxes, and contributions to his parish for its parochial school. The legalist retorted, "You should have such an expensive morality!" Moreover, it is no easy feat to live up to the line of legality without crossing it and becoming a criminal, especially as we have seen that no one knows where the line is located until the Supreme Court decides. Remember the ten different answers that the eight panelists gave to the tax question involving differences of millions of dollars in the amount owing. In such a society only the legalistically shrewd prosper, but more important, the others are prevented from being all they can be. When their spirit finally gives up the ghost, the society dies.

I believe Jesus makes this same point in Matthew 23:13. Does this verse not mean: lawyers prevent man from entering the kingdom of God because the exacting casuistry of the legalists makes it impossible for one voluntarily to obey the law of God? This passage comes immediately after that in which Jesus deplores man's following any leader other than God and that in which Jesus expressly forbids man's calling another man master or father. When Jesus thus confronted the establishment toward the end of his life, the society in which he lived was a theocracy, with its puppet secular activity under the remote control of the Roman Empire. This society had no Bill of Rights, no First Amendment rights, no first clause thereof reading: "Congress shall make no law respecting an establishment of religion, or prohibiting the free exercise thereof." Yet despite this great advance of ours, I find my country in the same condition that Jesus found his country. Plus ça change, plus c'est la même chose. So what should we do? If we are to follow the way of Jesus, we must tackle the jugular as he did, using the advances civilization has given us during the intervening years. Here we go again.

In discussing the article on the judiciary in my constitution for the world, I concluded that people still viewed the activities of judges differently from the way they viewed those in the executive and legislative branches of government. I suggested that realistically, ever since the law lost its peg to natural law derived from God, the law had become a myth in which many believe. In a 1947 case in which the Supreme Court indicated a minor return to natural law, Justice Holmes wanted no part of "this brooding omnipresence in the sky." I agree with the jurist if by his fluent circumlocution he meant that he did not want man's law to purport to follow the will of God. But when people believe in and are satisfied with the fundamental goodness of a system that allows nine people appointed by politicians to force their views about the problems of society upon all people, they make a religion out of the law. They certainly cannot believe that the deciding majority are so imbued with superior wisdom that these judges can do justice all by themselves on all the complex matters that come before them, matters so diverse that these judges cannot possibly be regarded as experts in all the fields of knowledge involved. Would those who believe that the standard for what government does should be justice have me believe that these few jurists, these system preservers, can render justice? Would they have me regard these judges' pronouncements, like those from a controlling superhuman power, as entitled to obedience and reverence? For God's sake, just as Japan's emperor agreed in 1945 that he was no longer God, the final significant defanging of an executive, let us now defang the judiciary and put this myth of the law to rest.

Fortunately, we have our wheel in place. It is the establishment clause of the First Amendment. Let us, therefore, hasten to disestablish this new religion. We have a wealth of precedents to help us. Under the doctrine of the separation of church and state, aid to parochial schools has been prohibited and prayers and Bible reading have been prohibited in public schools. As belief in the justice of the law is a religion, our position is simply that Congress can pass no law establishing this religion. Any law passed in the name of justice breaches the wall of separation of church and state and, hence, is unconstitutional. The only constitutional law is one that is a necessary evil. If God's book cannot be read in public schools so justice, God's law, should not be mentioned in public government. Litigation and legislation to achieve this disestablishment would also be evil, so I would oppose it as unnecessary.

Far worse than supporting governmental activity in the name of righteousness and justice, however, because subtler, are the unholy cooperative alliances between the mandatory and the voluntary communities. These communities can never work together successfully. Their standards are different. Necessity is an exceedingly poor standard. Anything can be done under the guise of necessity. Remember our general who blew up the infiltrated friendly Vietnamese village. His comment was: "I had to destroy it to save it." Beware, therefore, when the politician says it is necessary for the state to help the private sector and when the churchman says it is right for the private sector to help government. Just as an ayatollah wearing both miter and crown is the most primitive violator of the doctrine of separation of church and state, so in our sophisticated civilized society anyone who forgets that the government, motivated by necessity, and the church, motivated by righteousness, cannot work together is the most advanced violator of the doctrine of separation of church and state. Remember Fifi, and always keep the functions of these two communities separate, no matter how difficult. Sort them out in your mind and then in your practice. The mandatory community diminishes the person. The voluntary community fulfills the person. And never the twain should meet. The philosophers will understand this. The theologians can implement this. Together the brightest and best can show us the way to the future.

I have intentionally not illustrated these sophisticated violations of this doctrine of separation. Serpentine wisdom could do so, but then it might sow the seeds for more "necessary evils." The scriptural encouragement of serpentine wisdom is limited to enabling innocent children to enter the kingdom of God. One unsophisticated such violation, however, will serve as an all-sufficient illustration, namely: there are no spiritual ripples from one's doing something, otherwise good, if it gives one a tax deduction. The mere appearance or thought of filthy lucre (another necessary evil) takes God out of the relationship between giver and receiver.

Until the kingdom comes there will be a continuing battle between the two sectors—the public and the private. Let both beware of fraternizing with the enemy. Realizing that everything belongs to God, let us render unto Caesar the evils we reluctantly believe to be necessary and at the same time ask God for forgiveness. I believe we will receive his grace, his concurrent forgiveness. Finally, let us conclude with a bit of serpentine understanding of the word: When the pub(l)ic sector seduces the private(s) or when the private(s) tempt the pub(l)ic, their offspring is ultimate futility.

* * * * *

The next two chapters are summations of the peroration of this chapter. The first, structured within the confines of the book's second undelivered sermon, is a romantic summation for believers. We have seen how Jesus, in putting the myth of the law in its proper place, gives us the transcendent myth of the spirit. In this sermon I find Jesus to be the perfect paradigm of my paradox: the importance of one's being able to integrate completely his own religious and political thinking without endangering what today we know as the beneficient doctrine of the separation of church and state. The second chapter is a logical summation for nonbelievers in the form of a short entry from my diary of years ago.

Zeitgeist prompted my writing the sermon in what is currently called all-inclusive language, in the hope that this would increase the appeal of the chapter. In doing this I found it extremely difficult to find asexual words, especially asexual pronouns. I also found it cumbersome to the point of illiteracy to write "he and she" or "she and he" or "him and her" or "her and him" when in my day, in context, "he" always included she and "him" her and "mankind" everybody. So I am not now going to edit all of my sexist references out of the other parts of this book. In defense I suggest that, as the book is one long complaint about man's past treatment of religion and politics, men were probably the ones at fault and women should be happy if they perceive their noninclusion. Furthermore, this Zeitgeist, which I hope is just that, is no big deal for the reasons set forth in chapter 5, "The Family."

Chapter XIV
The Politics of Jesus

No one is an island. Throughout history thinking people have found their primary mainland in religion and in politics. In religious circles much has been said of Jesus. His politics, however, are far more exciting. He told his followers to seek the kingdom of God. Today some still call him Christ the King. What kind of kingdom was his? How long was his reign? Like many politicians who try to, Jesus helped the underprivileged. It was in them that he found the base for his support during three years of successful campaigning in the provinces. When he finally arrived at the seat of the local government, amidst the cries of his supporters and of the multitudes for him to proclaim his kingship he backed off and within the week he was executed for his failed coup. He never reigned. He had no kingdom. Yet, in failing, he shows the world the type of government we should seek.

Two of the followers of Jesus give us an insight into his political activity. When Jesus enters the scene at the age of thirty, the old leader, John the Baptist, recognizing the lad's potential, graciously steps aside. Thereafter, Jesus allows his followers to view him as their long-awaited leader. People are always longing for a just governor and always squealing because God lets such bad things happen. But just as political leaders expect loyalty from their followers, so followers expect loyalty from their leaders. So when the early campaign, though successful, produces no political victory, John from jail impatiently asks if Jesus really is the one to lead them, and Jesus has John told to look at Jesus' accomplishments, the reply of a politician. Judas becomes even more impatient than John has been. After all, he has a three-year investment in the campaign; so he tries to prod Jesus into action. Maybe Judas feels betrayed—and that after the way he has seen Jesus attract multitudes yet avoid them, Jesus certainly should be able to handle a handful of soldiers in a comparable fashion. In any event, Judas's kiss of death terminates the political life of Jesus, and before a hundred years have passed the religionists substitute the concept of everlasting life for that of the kingdom of God, a kingdom that during Jesus' lifetime at least two of his followers were thinking of in terms of this world.

The key to the political vision of Jesus is found in two of the remarks Jesus makes to the multitudes about John the Baptist just after John had questioned Jesus' leadership. Jesus says, Though John is a great man, he that is least in the kingdom of God is greater than John. Jesus further says, From the beginning of our campaign to seek the kingdom of God, the violent have taken it by storm. To these two clues add two parables, that of the lost sheep and that of the workers in the vineyard, and from these clues and parables one can envision the form the kingdom of God is to take. Let us try to.

First, the government cannot be maintained through force. This eliminates all forms of national governments that the world has yet seen as these, whether kingdoms, theocracies, tyrannies, dictatorships, socialist republics, or democracies, all need ultimatums, edicts, decrees, laws, rules, and regulations, enforced either by armies or by all sorts of constabularies. The bottom line in the workings of all these past and present forms of government is that the threat and the presence of brute force alone make them viable. Only leaders who are willing to use violence can take control of such kingdoms.

Secondly, the government cannot require a great, good, just, wise, or benevolent leader or governor, as have all the past or present governments that are generally considered to be relatively superior ones. Such a governor is responsible for all the people and to that extent relieves them of responsibility for their own development. Conversely, a general who deserts the troops in the midst of battle to look for and help a stray soldier should expect to be court-martialed.

But is it possible to have a government without leadership and without discipline? No, of course not. But one can envision a kingdom in which everyone leads only one's self, maintains an internal discipline, and voluntarily follows the norms. In such a kingdom the chain is no stronger than its weakest link. Therefore, the least is greater than he who looks for a great leader. Once one starts working for the kingdom one receives all of its benefits whether one starts early or late, and this is fair because one's starting changes a weak link in the chain into a strong link for the good of all. So the good person always leaves everything to raise up one lost sheep. In his botched kingship Jesus still lights the way to civilization's next higher form of government—self-government—a form of government the world has yet to see.

So there is the vision. Now would you like to know how you can start bringing to earth this kingless political kingdom of God? You will remember that Jesus allowed John the Baptist to preach that the kingdom of God was at hand. But the kingdom is not likely to come until there is an atmosphere on earth in which it can flourish. We can help create this atmosphere by always witnessing to the following three self-imposed commands, which I call the categorical imperatives:

The first imperative: Never speak of good government when referring to any of the forms of government the world has yet seen. Such governments have never and can never do any good. Such governments can do at most only what is necessary. For goodness springs from one's spirit, from love freely given and freely received, from the essence of one's being a creature of God. Necessity is merely a reaction to a problem that will not go away. External compulsion through force or through law or even through intimidation always diminishes people. It diminishes those who are helped by government, even when they are necessarily so helped, by depriving them of the love of the helper and of the ability to want to and to learn to help themselves. It diminishes those who pay for the help, because the power to tax is the power to destroy. It diminishes those who do the helping, as they became parasites preoccupied with the necessary and its required compromises and not with the good. I suppose many of you would now be willing to refer to just wars in terms of necessity and not in terms of goodness. But I would expect to find that probably not one of you would now be willing to refuse to call just laws good. We have a long way to go here.

The second imperative: Always speak of the good only in voluntary situations. Good deeds, voluntarily done and freely received, enhance both giver and receiver. This is the corollary of the first imperative.

The third imperative: Never confuse or mix these first two imperatives. For when the private sector and the public sector purport to work together, the private sector's acts become contaminated. They no longer have the potential of being freely done and freely received as pure and shining witnesses to the voluntary means by which the kingdom will come.

On these three categorical imperatives hang all of our hopes for a better world.

Note that these categorical imperatives do not tell us what to think or what to do about a single issue of the day. They only set forth the table manners that are to be used in handling the issues. For example, any discussion of legislation allowing or outlawing abortion should revolve around and be decided by whether the legislation is necessary, without mention of whether abortion is good or bad, right or wrong. Provided the table manners are followed, I leave to those involved in mandatory government the establishment of standards to guide them in applying the test of necessity to their actions, with one caveat. Although government can do no good, it can do varying degrees of bad, so each of us must be ever vigilant, like a wise serpent, to protect our liberty. Any discussion, however, of voluntary actions with respect to abortion should revolve around and be decided by whether they are good. So if our vision of self-government is to be fulfilled we must have some standard for deciding what is good and for establishing acceptable norms of conduct and we must have some institutional framework into which to integrate all of these individual voluntary acts. As it is the kingdom of God we are seeking, obviously the standard should be obedience to the will of God and just as obviously it is impossible for finite people to know the will of infinite God unless God wills it. This contradiction presents no practical problem, however, as all of this activity is to be entirely voluntary. All of us will be freely accepting the norms. So everyone will be determining that any suggested norm is not, to one's knowledge, inconsistent with the will of God. For this purpose history offers an abundant literature in which peoples have proclaimed the Word of God and there is a respectable body of this literature that is not inconsistent with the two great political visions of Jesus—no force and no intermediaries. Personally I try to find the will of God by meditating upon the person who created and controls the universe, by meditating upon the person of Jesus, whose obedience to the will of God was complete and by meditating upon the person who somehow works with and through the spirit of every one of us. And I look to the holy universal church to be the enabling institution to administer all of these voluntary acts. I suppose that some of you would be willing now to consider having schools and hospitals administered by the church rather than by the government, provided funds were available. But I would expect to find that probably not one of you would be willing now to have the church stop thinking and speaking about matters that are not the proper subject of thought and better left to God to take care of. Seeking the kingdom of God is a full-time endeavor. The church has a long way to go here. In my lifetime I have not seen the church anywhere make a conscious attempt to bring the kingdom of God to earth. Yet do we not pray, Thy kingdom come on earth, thy will be done on earth, as of course it is in heaven? And is this not why the cry of John the Baptist still rings true today: "Repent, for the kingdom of God is at hand"?

Seek ye, therefore, first the kingdom and righteousness of God here and now. There is no need to worry or concern yourself about anything else. God will take care of the rest.

Chapter XV
Jesus, Gamesman

When I left the ivory tower to enter the world there was a trilogy of books that were then having their brief day of fame in which the author, Stephen Potter, with devastating British humor, purported to teach the reader the art of gamesmanship. I offer for the uninitiate this example of gamesmanship: be sure you arrive several minutes late for a tennis singles match with an opponent who takes his punctuality pedantically. This is called the ability to one-up your opponent before the game has even begun. Potter's triology so impressed me that my diary entry for October 21, 1956, shows me applying his technique to an understanding of my religion. I reproduce this entry here as an anticipatory replication to those who have read my book and find it impractical. Some of you may sympathize with the book's fugue on the evils resulting from man's pushing his fellowman around. Some may appreciate the philosopher's emphasis on the concept of border crossings. Some may even agree that neither politicians, nor statesmen, nor judges, nor lawyers, nor civil servants can ever help us achieve the peace that passeth human understanding because pushing people around is the essence of their discipline and their work. But for such readers, as they put the fully read book down, their final thought will be expressed by one word: *impractical*. The diary entry that follows is solely for them.

Christianity is the supreme gamesmanship. The three important preliminary gambits that, when understood, explain the whole are:

1. Why would a perfect God create an imperfect world? Because he wants to give man a chance to make himself and his world perfect. How much more glorious a God who can create men who have within themselves the potential of becoming perfect! How much more successful a General Motors that could make cars that drove themselves!
2. How can man be saved when his imperfections prevent his meriting salvation? Simply by asking God for salvation. This is the whole point of having Jesus come down to earth, and himself not even be able to get out of the place alive. The proper terminology for this gambit include such expressions as *Grace of God, Jesus Redeemer, Justification by Faith, God so loved the world,* et cetera.
3. How do you get around the fact that you are really creating God in your own image and not vice versa? Two thousand years of precedents, which humbly I am happy to follow, said plunkingly.

After the student has mastered these three gambits, all that remains is for him to imitate the example of Jesus as revealed by Scripture, primarily in the three Synoptic Gospels and in Jesus' command: "Follow me." In passing let me point out that we may brush up against additional and technically important gambits such as that of the Holy Communion and the Holy Catholic Church, which might better be called institutional survival ploys.

It will, of course, take the student of gamesmanship some time before he will be able to grasp fully the fact that Christianity is the ultimate in gamesmanship. (The student of Christianity never will.) In this connection, I recommend placing a strong emphasis on fundamental principles. For example, always remember that the ultimate definition of gamesmanship is the art of avoiding being pushed around without lifting a finger. As the student grows into a mature gamesman he will acquire a great admiration for the British, admittedly the national past masters in gamesmanship, especially in their historical ability of getting others to fight their wars for them. But the minute the student comes to the fork in his learning where one way points to the cynic's knowledge that ultimately even the British must fight and the other way points to the Cross, then at that instant he is no longer a student. He then becomes a master in gamesmanship. Why? Because the gamesman cannot stoop to the use of crude physical force to prevent another from pushing him around. If he does he ceases to be a gamesman (see ultimate definition above). Then for the first time he sees clearly that teaching others through precept, example, and Socratic questioning to follow the Christ is the ultimate in gamesmanship and is the only supreme flawless method of avoiding being pushed around without lifting a finger. Admittedly, we gamesmen have been poorly practicing our art for over 2,000 years now.

Is this diary entry not the ultimate expression of serpentine wisdom? I caution the Christian not to be chagrined and not to view this diary entry as evidence of foot-in-mouth sickness. Remember, in our worship, we consider such lip service as a step in the right direction.

Chapter XVI
Final Play with Words

We have come to the ending for this book. My hope is you will have struggled through it with me and will be prepared to receive its serpentine wisdom. Whether or not you agree with any of it, I trust you have understood it. Lawyers are not insulted by people disagreeing with them, but by people not understanding them. Their professional competence depends upon their ability to be relevant and clear in expression. Here is a little game to see whether you have understood me. Pretend this book is a whodunit and tell me who was the brightest and best murderer of the spirit in my country in my lifetime. Who was the serpent? Read on and see.

But to those who by habit start with the last paragraphs of a book in order to see whether the author's conclusion is of sufficient interest for them to justify their spending time with it, I would mention that the purpose of the book is to find a better type of government, because in my lifetime ours has been rotten. Let us now see how both classes of reader—those who read this as the last chapter and those who read it as the first—like this old man's final punch.

The history professor in his final appearance before each freshman class always tied a piece of chalk to a string hung down the center of the blackboard, wrote "liberty" on one side and "security" on the other, and dramatically started the chalk swinging as he intoned, "Gentlemen, the lesson of all history is that from age to age the pendulum swings back and forth between liberty and security."

The vestryman from Hyde Park, however, thought for the good of the world he could control history as well as people through his use of words. "My friends," he said, "I give you freedom, four freedoms, freedom of religion, freedom of speech, freedom from fear, and freedom from want." Note how in the same breath he promised both liberty and security for the same time, because security means without care, and what more is freedom from care than freedom from want and fear? In my lifetime in my country he was the tempting serpent. We owe to him and his initiatives the weight of government that all of us carry, whether as a load on our back, as the Republicans say, or as a helping hand on our shoulders, as the Democrats say. Abuse of the word is a writer's greatest sin, his greatest separation from God, for "in the beginning was the Word, and the Word was with God, and the Word was God." Amen.

Appendix: The Constitution of the World

Preamble

We, the nations of the world, in order to form a government for the world that will insure international tranquillity, secure the common defense, promote the general welfare of nations, and provide the blessings of security to ourselves and our posterity, do ordain and establish this world constitution.

Article I: The Legislative Department

Section 1. All legislative power shall be vested in the world congress.

The World Congress

Section 2. The congress shall be composed of members designated by the several nations in accordance with the practice of each nation. No person shall be a member who shall not have attained to the age of thirty years and been nine years a citizen of the nation or of one of the nations from which he shall be designated except in the case of new nations.

Memberships in the congress, assessments in an amount equal to the annual budget of the congress and personnel quotas for the military forces of the world government, as determined by the congress, shall be apportioned among the several nations which may be included within this world government according to their respective assets in the manner herein set forth. The statement of assets shall be furnished to the congress by each nation before the first meeting of the congress and within every eighth year thereafter in such manner as the congress shall by law direct except that the congress shall accept each such statement of assets without question as to substance, shall not require any certification or appraisal, and shall request that all assets be valued at fair market value without deduction for any kind of debt, provided that land, excluding development thereon and including space above and below ground and water within the national territory, shall be included at fair annual rental values, and provided further that people shall be included at a per capita value uniform within each nation in such manner as each nation shall by law direct. Each nation whose annual assessment has been timely paid and whose military quota has been timely met shall be entitled to one member for each whole number resulting from the division of the stated assets of that nation by one-hundredth of the total stated assets of all of those nations whose annual assessments have been timely paid and whose military quotas have been timely met. There shall be no fractional representation except that each nation whose stated assets are less than one-hundredth of the total stated assets of all of those nations whose annual assessments have been timely paid and whose military quotas have been timely met shall be entitled, at its own initiative and expense and under procedures promulgated by it and approved by the congress, to join with such other neighboring and unrepresented nation or nations as may be required to attain a combined statement of assets of one-hundredth of the total stated assets of all of those nations whose annual assessments have been timely paid and whose military quotas have been timely met, and thereby obtain the right to designate one, but not more than one, member for such nations with the right to one vote for all purposes, provided that the annual assessment apportioned to one member shall have been paid in advance. The requirement that the nations so joining to obtain one membership be neighboring nations may be dispensed with on a case by case basis by a vote of two-thirds of the congress. Each nation's share of the annual budget is determined by the number of its members.

The congress shall have the right but not the obligation to elect from time to time to membership in the congress for terms of four years with reelections permissible, as representatives of all the peoples of the world, members or former members who have served in the congress for four years or more, to whom the membership requirements applicable to the other members of the congress who represent the several nations shall not apply, provided that the congress shall not have more than two such memberships outstanding at any one time, and provided that at the time of each such election by majority vote of the congress the members from each of the nations having the three largest number of members vote with the majority. The number of members in the congress shall not exceed one hundred and two.

The first meeting of the congress shall take place on the third day of January following the timely submission by all member nations of their statement of assets, the adoption of the first annual budget, the determination of the first annual assessments and of the military quotas, the payment in cash by the voting nations of their share of the first annual budget and their agreement to fill their military quota pursuant to successive revisions of the tax assessments and military quotas reflecting adjustments owing to nations not participating or participating jointly with other nations, and the award of memberships based upon such payments and agreements. Prior to the first meeting of the congress, these preliminary matters shall be conducted by an ad hoc committee composed of single representatives from China, Japan, the Union of Socialist Soviet Republics and the United States of America and a single representative chosen by the nations in the common market. Each committee member shall pay his own expense and his one-fifth share of the expense of the committee. Attendance at all meetings of the committee shall be open to one representative from each nation that within the time set by the committee submits its first statement of assets and agrees that its citizens and all persons present within its boundaries shall be subject to the jurisdiction of the world courts.

The above-mentioned ministerial matters shall be conducted by the congress every subsequent term of eight years at its expense and in such manner as the congress shall by law direct, provided that the congress shall approve the participation of any nation or of any combination of nations which was not in existence at the time of the immediately preceding award of memberships and the participation of any nation that had never become a member nation upon its or their submission of a statement of assets and an agreement that its or their citizens and all persons present within its or their boundaries shall be subject to the jurisdiction of the world courts. During any such eight-year period no change shall be made in the apportionment of memberships in the congress except that any nation or group of nations that does not pay in full its annual assessment in cash before the beginning of each such intervening year or timely fill its military quota shall lose its membership until the next eighth-year term when, without needing any approval of congress, it may again seek participation as a voting nation or a member nation by satisfying the applicable requirements but without having to satisfy any past requirements. Upon any such loss during any eighth-year term of payment of tax assessments or fulfillment of military quotas, the assessments and the quotas of the then remaining voting nations shall be proportionately increased; the increased assessment shall be paid in cash within thirty days of the reassessment, the increased military quota shall be timely filled, and additional memberships shall be awarded to such nations as are required to comply with the formula for determining the entitlement of each nation or combination of nations to memberships. The application of such formula may result in the award of more than one membership to a combination of nations until the next eighth-year term.

When vacancies happen in the membership from any nation or nations the executive authority thereof shall promptly fill such vacancies.

The world vice president shall be president of the congress but shall have no vote unless they be equally divided.

The congress shall choose their own officers and a president pro tempore in the absence of the vice president.

The congress shall have sole power to impeach and to try all impeachments. When sitting for that purpose they shall be on oath or affirmation. When the world president is tried, the chief justice shall preside; and no person shall be convicted without the concurrence of two-thirds of the members present.

Judgment in cases of impeachment shall not extend further than to removal from office, and disqualification to hold and enjoy any office under the world government, but the party convicted shall be subject to indictment, trial, judgment, and punishment according to the world criminal law.

Organization of the Congress

Section 3. The congress shall assemble at least once in every year, and such meeting shall take place at Geneva, Switzerland, and begin at noon on the third day of January, unless they shall by law appoint a different time or place.

Section 4. The congress shall be the judge of the qualifications of its members, and a majority shall constitute a quorum to do business; but a smaller number may adjourn from day to day, and may be authorized to compel the attendance of absent members in such manner and under such penalties as the congress shall provide.

The congress may determine the rules of its proceedings, punish its members for disorderly behavior, and with the concurrence of two-thirds of the entire congress expel a member.

The congress shall keep a journal of its proceedings, and from time to time publish the same, excepting such parts as may in their judgment require secrecy; and the yeas and nays of the members of the congress on any question shall, at the desire of one-fifth of those present, be entered in the journal. The journal of the congress and all other written materials of the world government shall be written in one language only, which the congress shall by law select, and except as to materials requiring secrecy all such materials shall be made available, but at the expense of the requesting party, provided that all such materials need not be written in the same language, the world president may select the language used by the executive department and executive orders shall also be written in the language of those to whom the order applies, and the world chief justice may select the language used by the judicial department and judicial opinions shall also be written in the language of any party bound by the decision.

Section 5. The members of the congress shall receive a compensation for their services, to be ascertained by law. They shall in all cases, except treason, felony, and breach of the peace, be privileged from arrest during their attendance at the session of the congress and in going to and returning from the same; and for any speech or debate in the congress they shall not be questioned in any other place.

No member of the congress shall be appointed to any civil office under the authority of the world government within five years of his retirement from the congress or to any civil office under the authority of the world government which shall have been created within eight years before the proposed appointment, or the emoluments whereof have been increased during such time; and no person holding any office under the world government or under any national, state, provincial, municipal, or other government shall be a member of the congress during his continuance in office.

Section 6. Every bill shall deal with only one general subject as indicated by its title and shall, before it becomes law, be presented to the world president; if he approves, he shall sign it, but if not, he shall return it, with his objections, to the congress who shall enter the objections at large on their journal, and proceed to reconsider it. If after such reconsideration two-thirds of the congress shall agree to pass the bill, it shall become law. But in all such cases the votes shall be determined by yeas and nays, and the names of the persons voting for and against the bill shall be entered on the journal. If any bill shall not be returned by the world president in twelve days after it shall have been presented to him, the same shall be a law in like manner as if he had signed it, unless the congress by their adjournment prevents its return; in which case it shall not be a law.

Powers Vested in the Congress

Section 7. The congress shall have the power:

(i) To prepare annually and timely a budget to meet the anticipated expenses required for the next year's operation of the world government as well as to reimburse the nation whose citizen is the world president for advances voluntarily made by it during the current year or during the immediately preceding year after the budget for the current year was adopted provided that the congress shall have timely approved or ratified such advances; and to assess such amounts at the beginning of each year from the voting nations in the ratio that their membership in the congress bears to the total membership excluding the two congressional memberships provided for in article I, section 2, and with appropriate adjustment at the beginning of each year to make allowances for nations who do not pay their assessment before the beginning of each year in legal tender of the nation whose citizen is the world president. The salaries of the members of the congress shall be payable annually in arrears after all other budgeted items shall have been paid. In the event of a shortage of funds or in an emergency the world president's nation may at the request of the world president advance funds which if approved or ratified by two-thirds of the congress before the next annual budget is adopted may be included therein for reimbursement. In the event funds are unavailable for any reason to carry on the world government except for payment of the salaries of the members of the congress the world president may resign in order to avoid criminal responsibility for failure to govern and the congress shall elect a world president from a nation willing thus to advance such funds until the next annual assessments are payable.

(ii) To regulate arms and drug traffic between the member nations and between member and nonmember nations.

(iii) To constitute tribunals inferior to the world supreme court.

(iv) To define and punish piracies and felonies committed on or under the high seas or in international air space, to define and punish trespasses vi et armis committed within the territory of any nation by aliens, and to define and punish trespasses with respect to air, water, and land pollution that extends beyond any national border.

(v) To repel invasions, contain insurrections, declare war, grant letters of marque and reprisal, and make rules concerning captures on land, water, or in the air.

(vi) To raise and support armies as herein provided.

(vii) To provide and maintain a navy and air force.

(viii) To determine from time to time, after consultation with the world president, the personnel requirements of the military establishment and to apportion such requirement among the voting nations in the same fashion as the amount of the annual budget is apportioned in accordance with the provisions of subsection 7 (i) of this article, provided that the congress shall approve the use of any personnel voluntarily offered by the nation of which the world president is a citizen in excess of such nation's quota.

(ix) To make rules for the government and regulation of the land, naval, and air forces.

(x) To provide for calling forth the militia of any member nation with its consent to execute the laws of the congress, contain insurrections, and repel invasions.

(xi) To provide for organizing, arming, and disciplining the militia of any member nation with its consent, and for governing such part of them as may be employed in the service of the world government.

(xii) To exercise exclusive legislation in all cases whatsoever over such district as may, by cession of particular nations and the acceptance of the congress, become the seat of the world government, and to exercise like authority over all places purchased from the nation in which the same shall be, for the erection of military and other needed buildings.

(xiii) To make all laws which shall be necessary and proper for carrying into execution the foregoing powers and all other powers vested by this constitution in the world government, or in any department or officer thereof, and to investigate the facts reasonably necessary to make such laws.

Restraints, World and Nation

Section 8.

(i) The privilege of the writ of habeas corpus shall not be suspended in the world courts, unless when in cases of war, rebellion, or invasion the public safety may require it.

(ii) The congress shall pass no bill of attainder or ex post facto law.

(iii) The world government shall have no power to levy troops or taxes, coin or borrow money directly or indirectly, enter into contracts except in the ordinary course of business and except as funds required by such contracts, including contingencies, have been included in an approved and published annual budget, or expend funds except from the treasury and for purposes designated in such budget or from advances voluntarily made by the nation whose citizen is the world president.

(iv) No title of nobility shall be granted by the world government and no person holding any office under it shall accept any emolument, office, or title of any kind whatever from any nation or any person.

(v) All sovereignty is reserved to each nation except as expressly delegated to the congress, the world president, or the world courts by this constitution.

Section 9.

(i) No nation shall enter into or remain in any alliance or confederation with another nation except as may be required to obtain joint representation in the congress pursuant to section 2 of this article and procedures approved by the congress, and no nation shall enter into any treaty with another nation with respect to mutual defense, arms shipments or any other military matter, or drug trafficking.

(ii) No nation shall, without the consent of the congress, keep armies, navies, or air forces in time of peace, enter into any agreement or compact with another nation with respect to military matters or drug trafficking, or engage in war, unless actually invaded or in such imminent danger as will not admit of delay.

(iii) Except in the case of criminals or those involved in legal proceedings, no nation shall prohibit or refuse a request for emigration, provided the person requesting emigration has been accepted as a first-class citizen by the nation where he proposes to reside.

Article II: The Executive Department

Section 1.

(i) The executive power shall be vested in a world president. He shall hold his office during the term of four years and, together with the vice president, chosen for the same term, be elected by the congress at its first meeting as its second order of business after first approving its own membership and at the first meeting of every fourth year thereafter. Before his election the president shall be the senior member of the representation of a nation holding itself at least one membership in the congress and the vice president shall be the next senior member of such nation's representation, but if there be only one member of such nation's representation, such nation shall make known to the congress in advance of the election the name of one of its citizens to be candidate for vice president.

(ii) Except in the case of new nations, no person shall be eligible to the office of president or vice president who shall not be a natural born citizen of the nation he represents and a citizen thereof for fourteen years; and no person shall be eligible to these offices who shall not have attained to the age of thirty-five years. The president and the vice president shall be from the same nation. Either or both may be reelected one or more times. Promptly after the election the president and the vice president if a member of the congress shall resign their memberships in the congress and the nation whose representatives they were shall fill such vacancies.

(iii) In the case of the death of the president, the powers and duties of the office shall devolve upon the vice president, who shall become president, and the nation whose representative the former vice president was shall with the advice and consent of the congress appoint a vice president to fill out the remainder of the four-year term. In the case of the inability of the president for reasons of health as declared by the congress to discharge the powers and duties of the office the same shall devolve upon the vice president until the congress removes such disability or declares the vice president to be president, in which case a vice president shall be appointed, as in the case after the death of the president. In case of the removal of the president from office by reason of impeachment, failure of the nation whose citizen he is timely to pay its annual assessment or fill its military quota, or resignation, the offices of both the president and the vice president shall be declared vacant by the congress, who shall forthwith elect one of their members to be the president for a term of four years commencing immediately together with a vice president following the procedures and requirements prescribed for the election of the first president and vice president.

(iv) The president and the vice president shall, at stated times, receive for their services a compensation which shall neither be increased nor diminished during the period for which they shall have been elected and they shall not receive within that period any other emolument from the world government, any nation, any person, or any entity.

(v) Before the president enters on the execution of his office, he shall take the following oath or affirmation:

> I do solemnly swear [or affirm] that I will faithfully execute the office of the world president, and will, to the best of my ability, preserve, protect, and defend the world constitution.

Section 2.

(i) The president shall be commander in chief of the armed forces of the world government and of the militia of the member nations when called into the actual service of the world government. The president shall locate such forces, their weaponry, and their transports in different places throughout the world giving consideration to locations in member nations whose stated assets are great, to proximity to unstable areas, and to the safety and strategic importance of the locations, and shall appoint as commander of each such location reporting to him a citizen of the nation in whose territory the military base is located. The president shall at all times have the power to inspect military facilities in member nations.

(ii) With the advice and consent of the congress, the president shall have power to:

(a) Create executive departments which shall have no rule-making authority except such as the congress shall grant and no adjudicative authority except such as the world supreme court shall grant.

(b) Make all executive and judicial appointments, provided that, except for the members of the supreme court, such appointees are citizens of the nation in which their duties are primarily performed and provided further that the president alone may terminate any executive appointment.

(c) Fill all vacancies that may happen during any recess of the congress or during the time the congress is deciding whether to consent or to withhold consent.

(d) Make treaties with, and appoint ambassadors and other ministers to, nonmember nations, provided two-thirds of the congress present concur.

(e) Grant reprieves and pardons for offenses against the world government except in cases of impeachment.

Section 3. The president shall from time to time give to the congress information as to the state of the world government including information with respect to the size, cost, and location of the military bases and the personnel requirements of the military, and recommend to the consideration of the congress such measures as he shall judge necessary and expedient; he may on extraordinary occasions convene the congress; he shall receive heads of state, ambassadors, and other public ministers; he shall take care that the laws be faithfully executed, and shall commission all officers of the world government.

Section 4. The president, vice president, and all officers of the world government shall be removed from office on impeachment for, and conviction of, treason, bribery, other high crimes and misdemeanors, or on permanent debilitating illness.

Article III: The Judicial Department

Section 1. The judicial power of the world government

shall be vested in one supreme court, and in such inferior courts as the congress may from time to time ordain and establish. The judges of the supreme court shall hold their offices during good behavior and as long as the nations of which they are citizens remain voting nations. The judges of the inferior courts shall hold their offices during good behavior and as long as the nations of which they are citizens remain voting or member nations. All judges shall, at stated times, receive for their services a compensation which shall not be diminished during their continuance in office. The supreme court shall consist of ten judges each of whom shall have attained to the age of forty-five years and shall have had at least five years' experience sitting on the highest court of the nation of which he is a citizen, and not more than three of whom at any one time shall be citizens of the same voting nation or of the same group of nations holding a joint membership.

Section 2. The judicial power shall extend to all cases arising under this constitution, the laws of the world government, and treaties made, or which shall be made, under their authority, provided that such controversies shall be between the world government and a member nation or nations, between two or more member nations, between the world government and officers or former officers of the world government or members or former members of its military forces, between nonmember nations as complaining party and the world government in cases involving treaties, between the world government as prosecuting party and any person as defendant accused of treason as defined in section 3, of article IV, crimes as enumerated in subsection 7 (iv) of article I, drug trafficking, or failure in his capacity as executive authority of a voting nation to fill a vacancy in its representation in the congress within the time specified by the congress, and between any aggrieved person as complaining party and the world government in cases involving the bill of rights in article VII.

In all cases the supreme court shall have original jurisdiction with such exceptions and under such regulations as the congress and the supreme court shall make.

The trial of all crimes except in cases of impeachment shall be by jury; and such trial shall be held in the member nation where the said crime shall have been committed except where safety may require a change of venue, but when the crime was not committed within any member nation, the trial shall be at such place or places as the congress shall by law direct. Except in criminal cases, the parties to the controversy shall each deposit with the court at the commencement of the proceeding an amount sufficient to cover its entire cost to the world government and at the conclusion of the proceedings the party in whose favor judgment is entered shall be given back his deposit without interest.

Article IV: Relation of the World Government to the Nations

Section 1. New nations may be admitted by the congress into the world government, provided that no new nation shall be formed or erected within the jurisdiction of any other nation, nor any nation be formed by the junction of two or more nations or parts of nations without the consent of the legislatures of the nations concerned, as well as of the congress, and provided further that no admission as a voting member shall take place until the next eighth-year apportionment of voting memberships resulting from adjustments required after the timely filing by the nations of revised statements of assets.

Nations who timely file declarations of stated assets and who agree that their citizens and all other persons while present in their nations shall be subject to the jurisdiction of the world courts shall be considered to be member nations entitled to the benefits and subject to the burdens of the world government except for the payment of assessments and the fulfillment of military quotas. A person charged with treason or other crime against the world government who shall be found in any member nation shall on demand of the world president be delivered up to the world court having jurisdiction of the crime.

Section 2. The world government shall not guarantee to any nation its national existence, but it shall protect each member nation from invasion and, upon its request, against interference in its domestic affairs through acts of violence committed by foreign nations.

Section 3. Treason against the world government shall consist in engaging in war, acts of war, or acts of violence committed against the world government or against member nations or their citizens or subjects by the citizens or subjects of other member or of nonmember nations, and in giving overt physical aid and comfort to the perpetrators of such acts. No person shall be convicted of treason unless on the testimony of two witnesses to the same overt act, or on confession in open court. The congress shall have power to declare the punishment of treason, but no attainder of treason shall work corruption of the blood or forfeiture, except during the life of the person attainted.

Article V: Provisions for Amending the Constitution

The congress, whenever two-thirds of its membership shall deem it necessary, shall propose amendments to this constitution, or, on the application of two-thirds of the voting nations, shall call a convention of such nations for proposing amendments, which in either case shall be valid to all intents and purposes as part of this constitution, when ratified by three-fourths of the voting nations, provided, however, that nations combining to hold one voting membership shall be counted as only one voting nation and provided further that no nation whose former member holds a congressional membership may vote on any amendment which seeks to increase the number of congressional memberships.

Article VI: Supremacy of the World Government

(1) This constitution and the laws of the world government which shall be made in pursuance thereof and all treaties made, or which shall be made, under authority of the world government, shall be the supreme law of the member nations; and the judges in every member nation shall be bound thereby, anything in the constitution or laws of any nation to the contrary notwithstanding.

Pledge—Tests

(2) The members of the congress and the members of the legislatures of the member nations and all executive, judicial, and military officers of the world government and of the member nations shall be bound by oath or affirmation to support this constitution; but no religious, educational, racial, or sexual test shall ever be required by the world government as a qualification to any office or public trust under the world government. No person shall hold

any office, civil or military, under the world government who having previously taken an oath to support the constitution shall have engaged in insurrection or rebellion against the same, or given aid or comfort to the enemies thereof, but the congress may on two-thirds vote of its membership remove such disability.

Article VII: The Bill of Rights

Section 1. The congress shall make no law respecting an establishment of religion, education, or economic system, or respecting a provision of health or welfare services, or prohibiting the free and open exercise of religion or education, or abridging the freedom of thought, speech, or publication, or requiring military service except of such personnel as the member nations may furnish.

Section 2. A well-regulated military being necessary to the security of each member nation, the right of each member nation to keep such a militia for such purpose shall not be infringed upon.

Section 3. No soldier shall, in time of peace, be quartered in any house without the consent of the owner; nor in time of war but in a manner to be prescribed by law.

Section 4. The right of the people to be secure in their persons, houses, papers, and effects, against unreasonable searches and seizures, shall not be violated by the world government, and no warrants shall issue but upon probable cause supported by oath or affirmation, and particularly describing the place to be searched, and the persons or things to be seized.

Section 5. No person shall be held in the world courts to answer for a capital or otherwise infamous crime, unless on a presentment or indictment of a grand jury, except in cases arising in the land, naval, or air forces, or in the militia when in actual service in time of war of public danger; nor shall any person be subject for the same offense to be put twice in jeopardy of life or limb; nor shall be compelled in any criminal case to be a witness against himself, nor be deprived of life, liberty, or property without due process of law; nor shall private property be taken for public use, without just compensation.

Section 6. In all criminal prosecutions in the world courts the accused shall enjoy the right to a speedy and public trial by an impartial jury of the member nation and district wherein the crime shall have been committed, which district shall have been previously ascertained by law, and to be informed of the nature and cause of the accusation; to be confronted with the witnesses against him; to have compulsory process for obtaining witnesses in his favor, and to have the assistance of counsel for his defense.

Section 7. Excessive bail shall not be required in the world courts, nor excessive fines imposed, nor cruel and unusual punishments inflicted.

Section 8. The enumeration in the world constitution of certain rights shall not be construed to deny or disparage others retained by the member nations and their peoples.

Section 9. The powers not delegated to the world government by the constitution, nor prohibited by it to the nations, are reserved to the member nations respectively, or to their people.

NATIONAL INCOME AND SOCIAL ACCOUNTING

Economics

Editor

SIR ROY HARROD

F.B.A.

Hon. Student of Christ Church, Oxford,
and Hon. Fellow of Nuffield College